The Roots of My
OBSESSION

The Roots of My

Thirty Great Gardeners

OBSESSION

Reveal Why They Garden

Thomas C. Cooper, Editor

TIMBER PRESS
Portland | London

CONTENTS

Introduction
Thomas C. Cooper

There are at least thirty reasons that people end up as gardeners. The essays that follow are proof of that. In fact, the motivations are far more numerous. A few folks seem born with a seed clutched in their fists; others make the choice deliberately, having ruled out banking or triathlons. But for most people, including the authors of this book, their transformation into gardeners is evolutionary, the result of years, often generations, of small unnoticed actions, the way a piece of land is shaped by wind, rain, sunshine, and the antics of man, until it has been changed entirely. The accounts in the pages beyond, by many of today's finest garden writers, are portraits of that metamorphosis.

I was raised on a strain of gardening that combined the minor virtues of engineering, math, Cold War chemistry, and internal combustion. My parents were a part of the victory garden generation, raised in an era when farming touched most recent family histories, and those who had some land naturally grew food and flowers as part of their genetic makeup, not as an exercise in outdoor decorating. People were comfortable with the land and the tools for working it. Families had Ball jars on their shelves and big freezers in the basement. A power outage meant more than losing an unsaved email; it put the summer's beet crop, stored in neatly stacked white cartons, at risk. Gardening was a tangible and often essential part of life, which was lived closer to the ground.

My father was the gardener in our family (my mother was the freezer, canner, and cook), and he was an active one. I don't know where he acquired the urge, although there was a family farm (with a water wheel and an Indian farmhand—he lived in a teepee, we were told) in Monsey, New York, some thirty-five miles northwest of Manhattan. It was a rolling, open landscape in the early days of the twentieth century, when lime was just gaining popularity. Whatever the instigating factors, by the time I was born my dad had developed a lifelong interest in tinkering with nature. Before moving from New York City to Vermont, my home ground, he had absorbed night courses in agriculture at Columbia University, owned and run an apple orchard upstate in Red Hook, and collected many of the USDA's yearbooks as well as a goodly library of their instructive bulletins

("Vegetable Gardener's Handbook on Insects and Diseases," "Potatoes in Popular Ways," "Mulches for Your Garden," and "Root Vegetables for Everyday Meals" among them). His copy of Maurice Kains's classic 1940 back-to-the-land primer, *Five Acres and Independence*, sat on a bookshelf behind his desk, ready for consultation and an inexhaustible source of inspiration.

With schooling as an engineer and a farmer, my father envisioned a garden as something carried out on well-tilled, rock-free ground (to the degree that condition can be achieved in northern New England, where stones rise up endlessly), rows aligned with all the precision a theodolite could impart, and seeds planted at exact intervals according to a notched sugar maple yardstick. A garden could contain many crops, but it ought to be square and true. Its supports should be tall and strong. Ours were made of oak shafts rejected for use in the construction of surveyors' tripods. We set their holes with a crowbar and drove them home with a five-pound sledge. The rows of beans and peas ran straight, the chicken wire taut.

There were actually two gardeners in my household. The other was James Underwood Crockett, the kindly gentleman who gained fame (among gardeners) in the mid-1970s as the down-to-earth host of PBS's *Crockett's Victory Garden*, as the show was originally called. Whether on TV or in his several gardening books, what

Crockett said went, from how deep to plant an asparagus root (eight inches) to when to apply the diazinon
(he was a firm believer in "better living through chemistry"). When he switched tomato varieties, we did too.
His books sat on a bookshelf in the kitchen for ready reference. Well after his death, when my wife and I moved
to our current home, my father built us one of Crockett's three-bin "Brown Gold Cadillac" composters as a
housewarming present.

My role in our family's gardens was as a farmhand,
picking out rocks and tossing them into the black plastic buckets stationed at the row ends, harvesting peas
or corn to take in to my mother for processing, pulling weeds. As my brother and I grew we took on mowing duties, wrestling a massive two-winged Locke reel
mower around the lawn as it threw up a spray of clip-
pings that released the fresh scent of summer and turned
your sneaker toes green. The mowing was followed
by trimming work with the hand clippers (a fiendish
device that I could only manage with two hands for a
number of years). Sometime in high school I took on
the Troy-Bilt rototiller, helping to keep the edges of the
asparagus bed fluffed and weed-free. I still admire a
crisply cut edge or a well-weeded stretch of soil almost
as much as I do a tapestry of perennials in full flight.

Some thirty years working among gardeners as an
editor added new tools and new approaches to my work

on the land. I discovered a world often without straight lines, generally without chemicals, one where flowers and vegetables shared equal billing. Any plant was fair game in achieving one's private paradise. The place where I grew up and still garden is overrun with lilac cultivars (my father's doing), but there is a heptacodium, a weeping katsura, and a Swiss stone pine.

Marketers have tried for decades to identify what makes a gardener in hopes of brewing up a large batch of it and sowing it, through advertising, across the land. It has never worked, and many who dreamed of getting rich by making gardeners have lost their shirts. Gardeners are a blend of family and geography, of childhood wonder and even sometimes the independence born of the parental "neglect" that allows a child to get lost in the woods, tracing the source of a springtime rivulet. They rise from trauma and travel. People come to gardening for the refuge of a personal Eden, endlessly complex in its makeup, gloriously simple in its demands.

The world of the small family farm and neat vegetable gardens carved into every backyard is fading rapidly. Some people lament this decline. Yet if one looks beyond the dense thicket of McMansions, there are plenty of gardeners carrying on with fruits and vegetables, trees, shrubs, and flowers. Their roots stretch back to Mr. Crockett and beyond—to plant hunters like E. H. Wilson, gardeners like Thomas Jefferson and Vita Sackville-West, layouts like the courtyards of Persia. Each story, like the ones in this volume, is different in its particulars—the disconcerting discoveries of an Irish childhood leading to the sanctuary of the greenhouse; love affairs with colchicums, alpines, orchids, or trees; a return to vegetable-growing; a lifetime raising fruit— but each is familiar in its goals and appreciations of a greener world.

THOMAS C. COOPER is senior editor at *Boston College Magazine*. He is also the former editor of *Horticulture* magazine and *The Gardener*. He has written for the *New York Times* and the *Atlantic* and is the author of *Odd Lots*. He lives in Watertown, Massachusetts.

Genetically Engineered
Tony Avent

Some folks fall into gardening, some are dragged into gardening, and a few others are born to garden. I fall into the latter category. There were a few marginal gardeners in my family, but no one with what I now recognize as a single-minded passion. Just as a computer comes with certain pre-installed programs, I was born with a fully functional 7.0 horticultural operating system, along with some specialized apps like an obsessive personality, an overactive imagination, an overly logical brain, and a touch of ADD. My dad did share my interest in plants (although our methods and standards for success were radically different). I remember poring over his gardening catalogs and accompanying him on trips to a nearby garden center, where I would harass the employees about misnamed plants while peppering them with other plant-growing questions.

Most of my non-school waking hours were spent hiking through the woods near our home, studying the local wildflowers. I became fascinated with discovering new plants and studying their habitats; along the way I developed an eye for species diversity, searching the woods for oddball forms of plants I already knew. At about age six, I began ordering plants through the mail, paying for my purchases with money from the wildflower terrariums I made and then passed to my parents to hawk at work. It was becoming clear: I could make a living from my love for plants. My dad deserves credit for recognizing that passion and cobbling a greenhouse onto our house. Before long, I was in the business of selling houseplants to the neighbors.

A significant event occurred a few years later when I asked my father to take me to Wayside Gardens in Greenwood, South Carolina. I'd scrutinized their beautiful catalogs over the years and assumed this must be the country's finest public garden. One weekend we made the four-hour drive to Greenwood, only to find no garden. There were a few beds of annuals, but that was it. Shocked and dejected, I listened as my father explained that most mail-order companies were not nurseries but simply shipping facilities. I decided that one day I would start my own mail-order nursery, with a garden that would never disappoint any visitors.

I wasn't very popular in high school, where an interest in plants was not something for a guy to admit in public, and when I got to North Carolina State University, I quickly gained a reputation as a plant nerd, the one to go to for plant-growing information. There were lots of questions; most of them, unfortunately, had to do with *Cannabis sativa*. But nerdiness did open some interesting doors. At one NCSU football game (I'm an avid sports fan), a gentleman behind me noticed the plant catalogs I'd brought to read during halftime and inquired if I would be willing to replant some of his dish gardens. I agreed. It turned out he was the owner of the topless club just across the street from the university.

My first proper plant job fell into my lap when my cousin, who was the bookkeeper for the NCSU horticulture department, mentioned to my parents that the greenhouses needed a part-time worker. The job allowed me to learn about a wide range of tropical plants, and scavenging in the greenhouse discard bins quickly expanded my own burgeoning plant collection. The sales of these propagated plants helped cover my college living expenses. (I also struck a deal with a local pizza joint that allowed me and my friends to eat for free, as long as I furnished and maintained the hanging baskets in their dining room.)

During my last year of college, after I had married my high school sweetheart Michelle (who didn't like plants), I was approached by the local men's garden club to assist with planting some newly purchased shrubs at the NC State Fairgrounds. This outing led to my first full-time job—as landscape director of the fairgrounds, a position I held for sixteen years. I set out to turn the property, all three hundred and forty acres of it, into a botanical paradise. Spurred on by my college professor Dr. J. C. Raulston, I treated the fairgrounds as an extension of the much smaller NCSU arboretum (which now bears his name), filling the fairgrounds with plants propagated at the arboretum.

Michelle and I purchased our first home in 1979. We then added a small greenhouse and began selling houseplants from our driveway during the occasional weekend yard sale. Around then my interest shifted to perennials, and we started developing our quarter-acre garden into a plant collection, soon numbering more than eight hundred different plants. True to my long-standing desire to share our plants and garden, we began inviting neighbors and friends into the garden. The guest register became our first mailing list. We were amazed to come home from work and find that visitors from all over the world had stopped by.

By 1988, we had filled every nook and cranny of the small property, as well as the next-door neighbor's yard, with our modest hosta and perennial nursery. We knew it was time for our next move. That year, we purchased the first two and a quarter acres of our current twenty-two-acre property, and christened our new business Plant Delights Nursery, Inc. Nineteen thousand plants later . . . The rest, as they say, is history.

TONY AVENT is the owner of Plant Delights Nursery and Juniper Level Botanic Gardens in Raleigh, North Carolina. He is also an international plant explorer, a hybridizer of hostas, and a freelance garden writer and lecturer. He is the author of *So You Want to Start a Nursery*.

The Apprenticeship
Thomas Christopher

I remember that meeting with my undergraduate botany professor vividly, even now, more than thirty-five years later. I had made an appointment with this distinguished scholar to ask for his help in designing an independent study project on some aspect of horticulture, a subject that my Ivy League university didn't offer.

"Frankly, Mr. Christopher," he said, briefly looking up from the papers on his desk, "I consider [horticulture] about on a par with hairdressing."

What's wrong with hairdressing, was my first thought. My second was that I needed to be somewhere else. Within six months, I was. I talked my way into a spot in the School of Professional Horticulture at the New York Botanical Garden, even though my knowledge of the craft was limited to what I had gleaned from readings of ancient Roman agricultural manuals. That and what I had picked up working in my mother's garden as a child.

This proved to be not so bad a preparation. Even in the flush of adolescent certitude, I recognized that I knew nothing. That made me more willing to listen to the immigrant Italian and German gardeners who bossed me for the next two years. My undergraduate major in ancient history and literature gave me a head start on botanical Latin and some sense of the antiquity of the craft to which I was being introduced: another of my memories from that period is of the jolt I felt when I recognized a pocketknife recommended in a catalog as being suitable for a gardener; it was identical, down to the green color of the bone handle, to a folding knife I'd seen pictured in a book about ancient Roman tools.

My time at the botanical garden was also, however, a forcible introduction to the world as it is. The younger gardeners there, who had been raised on the streets of the Bronx, could not believe that anyone as clueless as myself had actually been to college. They explained to me, for instance, the mystery of the digital clock in the window of a local coffee shop. Why was it, I wondered, that though it was clearly broken—the numbers didn't advance as the minutes passed by—it was reset every day? With some pity they explained to me that the shop belonged to the local bookie, and that the clock exhibited the day's winning number for the Mafia lottery.

More importantly, I learned to look closely at nature in a way I never had in my botany courses. During the six months I spent working in the native plants and the rock gardens, I observed the plants progress from winter dormancy, to bud break, to full bloom. I learned their pollinators, who fed on the plants, and how to reproduce the conditions of their native habitats. The habit of letting nature inform has been fundamental to the more sustainable, environmentally respectful gardening that has become the central commitment of my work.

I gained many traditional techniques from the older, European-trained gardeners, though never to their satisfaction. I acquired the basics of grafting, for example, from Dominic, but never developed anything like his proficiency with a grafting knife. Dominic had come up through an apprenticeship in Italy, during which he had to repeat such tasks endlessly and at high speed until they became part of his muscle memory. I was spared that sort of tedium, but as a result will always be, in a sense, an amateur.

I also learned the basics of propagation, of starting all sorts of plants from seeds, cuttings, and divisions. That, more than anything else, has made each garden I have planted a species of time machine. Cuttings of conifers I rooted while a student have become considerable trees; I know because I periodically diverge from the direct route of business or personal trips to visit them. The first flowers to bloom in my yard every spring are snowdrops I dug from the garden of an early mentor right after I helped to carry the coffin at his funeral. Bill Owens lives on in those simple but precocious blossoms. Similarly, I cannot see a French marigold without feeling the presence of my son, who brought one home in a Dixie cup from his preschool. He had started that plant from a seed, which as far as I know was the only time my garden-averse child ever tried such a thing. His marigold bloomed in our garden and set seed, spawning a race of flowers that endured several years. They are vanished now, as is he. Though in the spring following my son's death, when I came upon a lone purple crocus blooming in a hayfield, for a minute his free spirit was right there with me. Right there.

This is for me the greatest power and attraction of gardening, the transcendence it yields at unexpected moments. Occasionally, when I excise a dandelion from the lawn with one of the patented weed-pullers I inherited from my mother, who, late in life, developed an insatiable appetite for gardening gadgets, I hear her telling me how the task should be done. When I plant a tree, I may see my father, still young, punching holes in the hard earth of a pasture with a digging bar, sweat dripping from his nose, his glasses slipping off, a bucket full of saplings resting in the shade nearby.

A physicist has told me that time is a dimension that extends as readily backward as forward, and that our inability to see what we think of as the past is just a peculiarity of our limited powers of perception.

It's only in the garden that I have ever felt myself escaping this perceptual constraint. Sometimes the experience takes the form of an instant so beautiful and rich as to move me, for a moment, outside of time. In others, usually while planting, the sensation is of jumping forward to glimpse the seedling grown large, the landscape as it will be. What I continue to prize most, though, are the reconnections with people, places, and times otherwise lost to me. That's a power of plants my old botany professor could never have imagined.

THOMAS CHRISTOPHER has been reporting on gardening and environmental issues for more than twenty-five years, writing for a wide range of publications including the *New York Times, Martha Stewart Living,* and Britain's *Daily Telegraph.* He is the author of *In Search of Lost Roses* and editor of *The New American Landscape.* He lives in Connecticut.

Taste Testing
Rosalind Creasy

My living room has very large windows, the better to see my garden. Sitting there in my favorite chair, I watch as hummingbirds sip from my tree fuchsia, bumble-bees hurry from blossom to blossom on the blackberry vine, and a cheeky mockingbird takes off with one of my blueberries. The backlit roses mingling with the scented geraniums look like stained glass. Few queens sit on a throne with such a special view. I would take this view any day over a gilt chair facing a thousand-year-old tapestry.

My father gave me my first bit of a garden when I was a young child. Along with it came bean seeds and straw-berry and tomato plants and the encouragement to do whatever I wanted. He also included me in his own gardening efforts. I was close to the ground, so I was in charge of finding the cutworms curled around his tomato plants. With every cutworm I found, he would whoop and holler; I felt like I had saved the family from starvation. He pointed out the first butterfly of the season and talked about composting and how things live on in a different form. Life truths were shared, and when you're one of four children and you get your dad to yourself, it's a special time.

Gardening took a back seat in my life for a while, but it seems inevitable that plants and gardens would one day become the center of my life and that I would champion edible landscapes. While my food choices were limited when I grew up in the Boston area in the 1950s, they expanded dramatically in the '60s. Between Julia Child, Joyce Chen, and both the readily available ethnic foods in my new California home and those I discovered while traveling around the world with my husband Robert, I developed an appreciation for a wide range of vegetables, fruits, and herbs—all of which I wanted to incorporate into my everyday cooking. I began to grow familiar edibles with a friend at her home, and then snuck a few more unusual ones into the sunny flower borders that had been the parking strip in front of our otherwise tree-shaded property.

Before I got into horticulture professionally, I worked for ten years as a full-time volunteer for the Sierra Club and the League of Women Voters, studying environmental issues. I learned to question everything. As a result, I went through my horticulture classes kicking and screaming. The instructors talked about using chemicals and toxins when I was most interested in how we could eliminate them, and they had me memorize lists of water-hungry fruitless plants when I wanted drought-tolerant choices for our arid climate and lots of edibles. At that time, it seemed few people in the garden world were concerned about these issues.

I started writing *The Complete Book of Edible Landscaping* in 1979. In my world travels I had seen edibles in decorative settings, and I was convinced that Americans needed to rethink how they looked at growing vegetables, fruits, and herbs. But edibles came with emotional baggage. Americans believed they belonged in the backyard, well out of sight.

Flying in the face of that dictum, for the last twenty-five years I have grown most of my edibles in my front yard. And even if I say so myself, I have a beautiful front yard. My dwarf apple tree and blueberry shrubs are surrounded with a short boxwood hedge; dwarf fig trees stand sentinel-like in large urns near the front steps; vegetables mingle with flowers in the planting beds; and the occupants of a formal-looking chicken coop set back from the street welcome visitors with a contented cluck or two. I can't imagine having a garden without my flavorful basil, tomatoes, raspberries, pomegranates, and, of course, the eggs—oh my, they are so much better than store-bought!

This garden, along with those of my clients and my friends, has given me the experience, and often the photos, to convince other gardeners to grow edibles in their "ornamental" gardens too. Through trial and error I've learned I can make edible plants absolutely stellar in the most snazzy of settings. It's not the plant itself; it's how you use it in the garden.

I've also learned from the children in my neighborhood. I discovered that a two-year-old can single out the ripe cherry tomatoes even though her mother is stymied; that there is wonder in a hand lens (spiders look like hairy monsters); and that corn plants are more fun to harvest when they are first festooned with streamers. I didn't always allow the neighborhood children to enter my garden. I was afraid they would trample the soil or pick flowers I wanted to photograph. But a year's worth of longing eyes and pretty-pleases wore me down, and now there is hardly a day that a child does not visit. Today, my five-year-old neighbor brought a handful of eggs to the front door with an admonition: "You know it's not good to leave the eggs there all day because sometimes they break and they [the hens] eat them." I was contrite, and agreed.

The Fourth of July is approaching, and five children, ranging in age from five to nine, will arrive with their parents in the morning. They'll bring kitchen shears, and we'll harvest the wheat heads from the little patch we have planted. There will be much chatter. We'll strew the heads onto a bed sheet in the driveway, and we'll all do the "tennis shoe twist" to separate the berries from the chaff. We then will take the wheat inside to grind before making the bread. Once more, "my" kids, a whole new generation of them, will present their still-warm bread to our neighbors at our annual block party. I wouldn't give a queen's ransom to trade places with anybody that day.

These days, I can marvel at how much both the cultural landscape and the actual landscape have changed in the years since I wrote my first book. Conference planners used to sandwich my lectures between talks on roses, lawn care, and dahlias to assure me of an audience. Now, I'm the keynote speaker and edible landscaping is the draw. Edible plants have finally taken their place among the royalty of gardening world, where I'm firmly convinced they belong.

ROSALIND CREASY is a garden and food writer, photographer, and landscape designer with a passion for beautiful vegetables and ecologically sensitive gardening. Her latest book is a complete update of *The Complete Book of Edible Landscaping,* now called *Edible Landscaping.* She lives in Northern California.

Spring Fever
William Cullina

APRIL 23. My favorite part of winter is spring. I endure the darkness, cold, and near complete absence of life and color in winter as if incarcerated—outdoor time being limited to short daily commutes to the massive woodpile, with occasional longer sessions with the snow weights. Indoors I plaster my cell with images of plants and gardens, and I track the expanding path of the sun on the sunrise/sunset table while figuratively scratching off the days until spring. As we reach the vernal equinox, I can almost taste the sweet dampness of warming earth. On outings to the finally dwindling woodpile, past shrinking mounds of snow, I steal a few moments to claw my fingers through the frozen crust in search of the small, pale heads of still-slumbering plants. Even this premature and precarious contact with life brings the spring fever to a delirious pitch that I can only liken to a sort of mania. If you garden in a place visited even briefly by old man winter, you know the symptoms—quickening pulse, loss of appetite, swelling confidence, and a delicious though probably unwarranted optimism that Life Is Back! This year, old man winter didn't just visit coastal Maine, he bought a house.

Thankfully, I write this sitting outside—on my porch, to be exact—listening to the incessant staccato trill of a dark-eyed junco harmonizing with whooshing wind blowing in from the ocean through the spruces. Unlike last year when it leaped nimbly in, spring has come painfully, trudgingly slowly this year, but it has come. The patches of *Hepatica transsilvanica* I raised from seed ten years ago are blooming electric azure, and the pass-along rhubarb from Melissa's great-great-grandfather has emerged from the dark chocolate compost my oldest son Liam and I spread just days ago. I am just as palpably jubilant (if less visibly so) as my naked, shivering son Ronan, who has just escaped from the tub and come streaking out onto the porch with a lunatic grin. At this time of year more than any other I am glad, no ecstatic, to be a gardener, waiting with mad anticipation for the return of old friends, back from their winter's retreat. For me frenzied, manic spring embodies everything I love about plants—color, life, rebirth, and the possibility that this year will be bigger, brighter, and more vibrant than the last.

JULY 28. Yesterday it happened. With everything finally planted, the weeds temporarily at bay, and the garden refreshed by rains after a long dry stretch, I reached that brief apogee in the arc of the season where I could sit on the bench and just appreciate. It is that magic time of year between the rising cacophony of spring and the slow murmuring descent of autumn when there is stillness in my soul. Right now, nothing needs doing. It has been the most frenzied spring yet at Coastal Maine Botanical Gardens, where I work—a season stretching well into summer. We planted just over twenty-nine thousand plants, and created four acres of new gardens. I have laid out so many plants this year that I started seeing them in my sleep—one pot after another plunked atop the freshly turned earth in endless triangles stretching off to infinity. At home, progress has been much more modest, but the front of the house is exuberant with bloom, and I did manage to grub out another seven hundred and fifty square feet of hard, stony ground near the woodpile for vegetables. It never ceases to amaze me how a pick axe, good compost, and a spading fork can turn the most life-forsaken ground into a fertile patch of tomatoes, pumpkins, basil, and carrots. We have passed through four horticultural time zones since I last wrote: bulb time, spring ephemeral time, peony time, and rose time. Currently we are in lily time, and the garden is truly redolent with the cake-batter musk of *Lilium* 'Brazilia', 'Golden Stargazer', and 'Silk Road'. Rich vanilla music blows from their trumpets like Miles Davis circa 1963, lulling me into a pleasant, stumbling stupor as I wander by. Daylilies, too, are everywhere apparent. Though they lack the cool sophistication of true lilies, there is no doubt that the optimistic transience of their flowers is a perfect counterpoint: John Philip Sousa meets Miles Davis. This time will be as fleeting as the others, but it is where I am now and I am grateful . . . content . . . relaxed.

OCTOBER 9. July seems so far away now. Contented summer has transformed slowly but inevitably into anxious, kaleidoscopic fall. The weather has been relentlessly lovely, with cool, brilliant days and dewy nights that have wiped away the green in favor of yellow, orange, and red. Though every summer I can't believe it, by September I am ready with a hearty welcome as fall tumbles though the garden gate. In New England, fall brings a sense of urgency that rouses me from my summer slumber. The arrival of the first goldenrod blossoms and the return of the cool dry northwest wind means there is much to do before the first snow blankets the ground. I have begun cutting back the perennials in earnest. I used to leave just about everything until spring, but the tumbled stems make a perfect palace for voles. So cut I must, a bit here and a bit there, as each plant retreats root-ward in its turn. Strangely enough, this gradual cutting back allows me to bid each plant goodbye—a pat on the crown for a season well done and a nod that says "hope to see you in spring."

Fall is a blend of melancholy, quiet celebration, and anticipation mixed with a slight, fluttering anxiety. I am sad to see the chlorophyll drain from the garden but also happy for this, the best garden year I have ever had. I can also already feel the excitement building for next spring. But there is that palpable worry about the approaching winter. Will the frosts come too early, will the snow arrive and leave too late, and most of all, will winter's merciless, numbing exhalations turn my gardens to blackened mush? And yet, for the moment, anxiety has been completely drowned out by the spectacle of fall. Thank you maples, thank you huckleberry, thank you ash, and thank you red oak: thanks for your anthocyanin, your carotenoids, and your flavonoids!

JANUARY 2. Inevitable January is here. My appeals have failed and my seasonal incarceration has begun. We had our first snowstorm a few days before Christmas, and I used the snowblower to pile an extra layer over some of my more tender treasures in the garden out front. We have not had any below zero cold yet, but that will almost certainly be here soon. It is so dark by the time I leave my office at 4:15 that I use the flashlight app on my phone to find my way to the car. I have been occupying myself with ordering plants for the gardens—an activity that brings me considerable distraction and satisfaction. I have also been catching up on labeling the 25,000-odd images I took this year. It is a fitting pastime for an inmate, spending hours gazing at friends and family. Happy times. For fun I just looked at images I took late last July when the lilies, hydrangeas, and daisies were all at their peak and tried to put myself back into the frame of mind I was in when I wrote the entry above. It is funny because although I remember it like I remember the plants themselves, I cannot for the life of me recapture that lazy, self-satisfied *feeling* of mid-summer. It is as if I am gazing on a painting of that moment done by someone else. I see it, I can relate to it, but I cannot live it.

In truth, my gardening life would be greatly diminished without winter. The blanket of snow puts the tangible parts of gardening out of sight and out of mind, so when each spring comes, it is the very first spring. Without winter, there would be no end—and no beginning. Last year's season would trail on into this like a dull conversation filtering in from the room next door and preventing me from sleep. Still, I can't wait for spring!

WILLIAM CULLINA is the executive director of the Coastal Maine Botanical Gardens in Boothbay. He is the author of many books, including, most recently, *Understanding Perennials*. He lives on Southport Island, Maine.

My Time Machine
Rick Darke

How many years does a beech seedling take to reach
forty feet in height? What is the lifespan of Jack-in-the-
pulpit? When will the spring air be scented by spice
viburnum, and for how long? Will redbud blossoms
retain their color for days after they've fallen? When
do great masses of red-winged blackbirds and grack-
les speed by overhead, their shadow patterns flicker-
ing on the ground? In what month will the rising sun
again paint the east-facing surfaces of tree trunks and
walls? I know the answer to all these questions because
I garden. Though anyone who gardens must pay close
attention to the spatial dimensions of place, many of the
greatest rewards of working with a landscape have their
origin in the temporal dimension.

My garden is my time machine. Unlike a clock telling
the passing time with relentless precision, the garden

is a complex instrument capable of marking time and also of influencing the apparent passage of time. Just as experiencing the landscape by bicycle reveals more than travel by car, and walking reveals more than bicycling, simply being in one's garden provides an opportunity to expand moments into minutes or incidental events into catalysts for contemplation. In this spectacularly technological age, when the only certainty is the accelerating pace of change, I welcome any device which motivates me to slow down. However, a really fine time machine is not dedicated only to slowing. Many events in the garden are extraordinarily rapid, so fleeting that you'll miss them with a sideways glance. The steady awareness necessary to observe such chance happenings can counterbalance the frenetic routines of contemporary living.

For much of my life I've held a deep belief in the value of revisiting. I've never wished to turn the clock back, but I find immense pleasure and inspiration in establishing points of reference and observing how individual elements either evolve or remain unchanged, and how my perception of them is affected by the inevitably shifting context. No matter how much a gardener intervenes, no garden is completely static, even for a short span of time. Close observation of barely noticeable changes has led me to an enthusiastic welcoming of this dynamic. My professional studies of local landscapes have taught me that they are the most influential to us, personally. This is true simply because we spend the most time in landscapes that are close at hand. Well, what landscape is ever more local or closer at hand than our garden?

If you garden on one property for many years as I have, you become aware of cycles that are anything but random or spontaneous, though they may have seemed so at first. The periodic cicada species, which visit at multi-year intervals, are a classic example. The flowering of our dogwoods isn't quite clockwork; however, it's a fair bet that a banner year for bloom will be followed by a subtle one. My wife and I take pride in matching plants to the conditions in our garden and measure success, in part, by how long they endure: many plantings are now well into their third decade without renewal on our part. Yet few individual plants live forever, and it has been valuable to learn the likely lifespans of herbs, trees, and shrubs and to understand their individual cycles in the greater temporal dimension of the garden as a whole.

Among my greatest delights are the garden's temporal links to the landscape beyond. When the new leaves of American beeches in the garden are turning that unique, fleeting, bright yellow-green, I know it's that time in the local woods, too, and that time is early May. It's mid-June now, and I saw my first firefly a couple of weeks ago—in the garden. This inspired me to look for fireflies in surrounding meadows and wood-land edges, and, sure enough, they'd arrived there too. I notice so many living phenomena first in the garden, then know to be watchful for them beyond its bounds. It's easy to miss the brief blooming period of bloodroots in nearby habitats, but less so if I've been alerted to this event by the plants growing at home. There's a low wet area edging the bottom of our property, and when we hear spring peepers begin their song there in late winter, we know to keep the windows open the next time we drive over the bridge that crosses the creek and its moist bottomlands.

My fascination with time and landscape has led me to create varied elements enhancing the garden's abil-ity to reveal temporal patterns. Twenty-three years ago, when I first arrived here, the eastern edge of the property faced out on an agricultural field that contin-ued to the wooded edge of the local preserve. I certainly knew how to locate east, but I had little orientation to the points on the horizon where the sun or moon rose in different seasons. I built a simple structure of red-cedar posts, held together by branch stubs and gravity, framing a fixed point of reference at the garden's eastern edge. It remained in place for more than a decade, and in that time it taught us details of the when-and-where of the sun and moon in our home habitat. Though not quite a successor, the next device was built from recy-cled sash vents original to Longwood Gardens' main conservatory, where I worked at the time. The sashes were made of cedar hand-sheathed in copper, with triangular glass panes in repeating patterns of eight. I set a number of sash sections on end in a small meadow area near the south edge of the garden, directly in line with the view from the main bedroom. The whole affair was positioned mostly perpendicular to the sun's and moon's arc from east to west across the garden. Many years have passed, and we have since learned to tell the time of year by the seasonally distinct patterns of solar and lunar illumination on the sashes' acid-rain-etched glass. It is surer than any sundial, more emotionally and intellectually accurate than any clock. It won't last forever, but for now it is an integral element in my garden, my time machine.

RICK DARKE is an author, photographer, lecturer, and consultant focused on contextual landscape design, planning, and management. His books include *The American Woodland Garden*, *The Encyclopedia of Grasses for Livable Landscapes*, and *The Wild Garden: Expanded Edition*. He lives in Landenberg, Pennsylvania.

Chaos Theory
Page Dickey

I love to weed. I realize this is not a universal senti-
ment, even among gardeners. But every spring I am
reminded how utterly happy I am on all fours, inching
along the garden beds, pulling out the culprits, scratching the earth with my three-pronged weeder, enjoying
the results as I look behind at my progress.

I know my enemies intimately. The rangy chickweed
that comes out in a satisfyingly intact cluster so long
as I dig my fingers in at its center before pulling; the
catchweed that sticks to my hand and stretches like a
rubber band. Our chickens relish these two creepers,
and therefore I save them in a separate bucket to take
up to the chicken yard at intervals. I know well the
persistent ground ivy that smells sharply of mint and
threads through grass and perennials just at the soil's

surface and needs to be teased out gently to get the long strands. The coarse-leaved dock requires prying with a knife to ease its hold on the earth. If, in impatience, I just pull the leaves, I hear the stems snap and know the long fleshy taproot remains in the ground, ready to leaf out again. The same is true of Japanese knotweed with its bamboo-like stems, and the waxy ribbed bouquets of broadleaf plantain, which lies flat against the ground, and also the jagged leaves of dandelion that litter our so-called lawn. If I miss pulling the tiny-leaved rosettes of white-flowering bittercress from the garden beds in early spring, by late May the seed will ripen and explode in my face when I pull the plants, and I know with a sinking heart that many more of these little devils will await me next year.

As my basket fills with the interlopers, my borders of perennials, shrubs, and vegetables are revealed and highlighted, the soil around them freshly stirred. On hands and knees, I become reacquainted with their beauties, the pattern and scent of their leaves, the shape of their flowers, the markings at their throats, the color of their stamens. This world of earthly details absorbs me. I think of nothing else—not the emails I haven't answered, nor the errands that need doing, not the state of the world, or how we are going to pay our taxes, or what I am going to wear to the dinner party in the city. My thoughts, my body, my whole being is concentrated on the feel of the earth, the look of the plants, on the vignettes that are being created through this basic sorting out of what is desirable and what is not.

Why is it that gardening gives me such elemental pleasure? Why does one person love to muck about in the soil and another abhor it? My sister and I spent our childhood in the same privet-hedged garden, both helped our father plant rows of corn, walked the grass paths among beds of tulips and summer phlox, ate the cherry tomatoes warm from the sun. All the while she dreamed of velvet dresses and a life on the stage, while I collected tadpoles and lovingly polished the leaves of my philodendron in a pot on my dormered bedroom windowsill. I got the gardening bug, and she did not.

I designed my first garden at age twelve in a small clearing in the New Hampshire woods where the septic tank for our summer house was buried. I scavenged granite stones to line the path leading to my circle and edge its rim, then filled it with flowers and ferns that I dug up from the wild all around me. Who knows why, but even then I felt the urge to gather plants into some sort of design imposed on nature, not content to enjoy these native plants in their natural wildness. And so today, I am not content to walk in the grassy fields that surround our property, but want my very own meadow, a native meadow at that, one half-acre of waving grasses, butterfly weed, asters, and goldenrod around the lap pool within our old fenced horse paddock. Is this easy to achieve? No! It requires an ongoing battle with alfalfa and clover, left over from horse days, as well as dock and wild lettuce, mile-a-minute vine, purslane, and ragweed. Am I going to give up? Absolutely not. I will weed the meadow.

Gardeners don't listen to easy. We want to tame nature, give it order, play with it and against it. The great modernist landscape architect Dan Kiley believed that gardens should be outright reflections of the hand of man, not artificial imitations of nature. "Man *is* nature, just like the trees," he once said. Those lines of fruit trees in high grass, the stripes of grape vines at the foot of rolling lavender-blue hills—isn't there something elementally appealing about that order imposed on the landscape, those straight lines played against nature's wildness?

For thirty years, I've attempted to achieve this sort of order at Duck Hill, our three-acre yard in old farming country just north of New York City. I use hedges to divide its space, clipping them to strict formal lines, then allow species roses to arch and weep, and crabapples to twist their branches, and sunflowers and Culver's root to wave against their controlled geometry. Most of the paths are straight, drawing your eye from one enclosure to another, but here too, I like those edges broken, a boxwood bulging out, cranesbills and pinks spilling, mulleins and poppies seeding outside of the beds. In our vegetable-cutting garden, I have neat rows of lettuces and beets and onions, but can't bear to rid the paths of all the larkspurs, hollyhocks, and Johnny-jump-ups that insist on congregating there. And so, as I weed, I think about editing, what transgressors I will allow to remain in order to achieve that sense of controlled chaos.

In the dog days of summer, when the sky is a white haze of humidity and the temperature hovers around ninety, when we haven't had rain in a week or two and the earth is cement-dry, I admit weeding is not so much fun. With joints stiff and aching, I think about napping instead, or reading a book. But in the early dew-moistened morning or at the quiet, dusky end of the day when the light is soft and slanted low, an hour or two of tugging weeds still brings happiness.

PAGE DICKEY has been gardening since her early twenties and writing about gardening for the last two decades. She lectures about plants and garden design and has written many articles for magazines over the years. Her garden, Duck Hill, has been featured in a variety of periodicals. Her most recent book is *Embroidered Ground*. She lives in North Salem, New York.

There Lies Peace
Helen Dillon

The only thing I'm really good at is worrying, and I spend most of my time in an advanced state of agitation. The moment some niggling little worry is dealt with, another appears. Making lists and crossing things off is a useful distraction, as are cigarettes, chocolate biscuits, and drink, which have all been a help in their day. But the main source of sweet and blissful peace throughout my life has been the garden, from my first encounter with a row of hyacinths under the hedge in my great grandmother's garden. I had to rush into the house—insofar as a toddler can rush—to demand that everybody should come outside to see what I had found.

My next gardening epiphany occurred when I was around eight, just after we'd moved from Worcestershire to Perthshire in Scotland. Standing in dappled shade at the edge of the woods behind our house, I looked up to the astonishing sight of a lone giant Himalayan lily (*Cardiocrinum giganteum*), its fragrant great white trumpets in full bloom atop a stout green three-metre stem. I thought at first that I was dreaming, and had to keep going back to see if the plant was still there—indeed it was, although the flowers, for which the bulb needs seven years from seed to blossom, lasted only a week or so.

That was a time of revelations for me. Every day I would play outside, mostly with the gardener's children, but suddenly this was stopped—I later understood this was to prevent me from picking up a local Scottish accent. At that time I also realized I was only a girl, and although the eldest, with two younger brothers, I could never inherit our family's lands or title. It was hard to accept the idea that girls are irreversibly second rate. I took refuge in the little patch of garden I had taken over. There was a winter jasmine and a few polyanthus, which I thought were quite wonderful. I also loved wandering down to the greenhouse, where I'd started a collection of regal pelargoniums that I still grow here in Dublin. Another place where I could find calm during the upheavals of a somewhat turbulent childhood was the clearing in the woods where wild daffodils grew.

At the risk of sounding smug and British, I enjoy any sort of gardening. I like digging, lugging buckets of compost, sweeping paths, rooting out dandelions, clearing drains, sieving leafmould. I like going into the greenhouse and picking up the bell-jar to see how the cuttings are getting on—which is often remarkably similar to how they looked the day before. I'm even happy washing pots, although I know I'm the last of the pot-washing generations. I learned my gardening from old gardening books, read with a flashlight under the covers, in which there were rules such as those requiring a gardener's boy to learn for seven years before being allowed to water the greenhouse.

Just being in a garden thrills me, no matter the time of year or the weather. In Ireland the light changes in fractions of a second. You can have a drab light, when the colour drains away and everything looks dull. I remember the late Graham Stuart Thomas, whom I greatly admired, came to my garden on such a day and remarked, "What very good maintenance you have." (I expect he was implying that there was nothing here of artistic consequence.) At that moment I agreed with him. Of course, as soon as he'd gone, out came the sun, and all was redeemed. Also the Irish air is never absolutely still, so plants are always mobile, and the water of the canal is often rippled by little waves.

I spend a lot of time moving plants to where I imagine they'll do better, propagating extras in case I lose them, rescuing those that are squashed, deadheading spent blooms, tweaking off scruffy leaves, and splashing plants with cooling water. The last thing I want in the garden is to be made to feel guilty, so if a plant is still looking unwell after a couple attempts to make it happy, off to the compost heap it goes.

I always flattered myself that I was beyond the influence of gardening fashions, but come to think of it I was making colour borders for thirty years (thankfully I've got over that phase) and as for using grasses and planting in drifts? No better woman. I'm also quite certain that I never want to set eyes on another ball of box.

My list of favourite plants is long and ever-changing. Today it begins with *Melianthus major* 'Antonow's Blue', *Romneya coulteri*, *Dierama pulcherrimum*, *Rosa* 'Phyllis Bide', *Crambe koktebelica*, *Ferula communis*, plus every sea holly you care to mention, but by tomorrow—you know the answer already.

Just being in a garden gives me incredible peace, like being in a foreign cathedral on a hot afternoon, when there's nobody around, only the sun beaming from high above, lighting up motes of dust. Somewhere I can gather all my thoughts and deal with them, slowly and quietly, one at a time.

HELEN DILLON's acclaimed garden in Dublin, Ireland, has been open to the public for more than twenty-five years. Much sought after as an author, broadcaster, and garden consultant, she lectures frequently in the United States and New Zealand as well as all over Britain. Her most recent book is *Down to Earth with Helen Dillon*.

Island Life
Ken Druse

I often wonder why I garden. I wonder when the rising river threatens my garden on an island in northwest New Jersey, or a new invasive species appears; in years of drought, and, less frequently, when weeks of spring rain turn the lilac blossoms to mush; when ice storms shatter the trees; when county road workers hack down the plants in front of the house; and when herbaceous perennials simply do not return after winter. I think about a quarter of the perennials I've bought over the years turned out to be annuals.

This area was rural when I moved to the island in 1995. The sound of the river was a constant, soothing companion. Today, the rushing sound is traffic. The house (an old mill store built around 1850) is one story higher than the garden, something I have come to appreciate. There is an eight-foot-high stonewall around most of the island: how charming. The wall, it turns out, was not only built to keep the soil in but the river out. I knew this island was a floodplain, and that there could be problems. But there are several old shallow-rooted trees here that would not have survived for long under water, so I figured buying this wonderful, eccentric property was worth the risk.

Since I arrived there has been the ten-year flood, the hundred-year event, and the millennial flood, when the governor called out the National Guard and the face of Sparta Mountain slipped down to close the highway for months. Most floods didn't last long. The majority happened in the late fall or early spring, so not too much of the dormant garden was disturbed.

But a few of the dozen or so floods stand out in my memory. There was a shallow, fast-moving one that scraped away big chunks of garden. There was a deep flood that didn't cause much damage, and cleanup amounted mostly to retrieving the wooden garden furniture and newly planted sweet birch saplings from the deer fence, where they had lodged. The worst flood dumped two feet of sand on most of the garden. I had to rent a backhoe.

One fall, it started to rain and continued through the next day. I put on my boots and went out to take some photographs when I noticed a telephone pole floating by. (You never know when you're going to need a telephone pole—it has since been cut in half for giant gateposts in the deer fence). I lassoed the pole with a garden hose and was tying it to a spruce tree when I realized the water was waist high and my camera and tripod had tipped over. The camera was ruined, but every picture came out.

One night I heard a loud crack in front of the house and ran out to discover that the seventy-foot-long planting of American Pillar roses, which were trained on swagged chains running between wooden posts, had vanished. Five hours later, a driver with rose canes sticking out of the grille of his new SUV was picked up for a DUI and charged with leaving the scene of an accident.

The latest problems have to do mostly with the new normal—soaring summer temperatures and record-breaking snowfalls. In August 2011, Hurricane Irene covered the garden with five feet of water and tons of debris. I was cleaning up when Tropical Storm Lee came through, causing much more damage that Irene and keeping water on the sodden landscape for five days. These were the worst floods in recorded history. Autumn color never came that year, and leaves were still on the trees on October 29 when twelve inches of wet snow came down and brought parts of many trees with it.

Despite all my trials, the first time I seriously thought about giving up had to do with a "new" weed: Japanese stilt grass. I could barely keep up with it; the government doesn't seem to care about this scourge that, in four short years, colonized all the roadsides. The weeds and browsing deer have wiped out the woodland understory faster than development in this formerly overlooked corner of the most densely populated state in the union. Gone are the trilliums that were here when I first walked the path through the forest. Gone are the goldenseal, the Dutchman's breeches, and the bleeding heart. I was ready to throw in the trowel.

I've been playing in the dirt for most of my life. My mother didn't garden much, but she loved nature, and one of my earliest memories is when she introduced me to a Jack-in-the-pulpit at the Trailside Museum. I was mesmerized. Our quarter-acre suburban landscape had respectable foundation plantings, plenty of lawn, and a few clusters of mature shrubs that had once been part of the landscape for a long-gone mansion. The ten-foot-tall rhododendrons and shaggy Chinese snowball bushes became my private forts and secret hideaways. I scratched roadways in the soil and bulldozed inch-high piles of leaf litter.

My conversion from earthmover to gardener happened when I discovered the joy of nurturing plants. I've always been drawn to puppies, kittens, infant snakes, baby birds, and orphaned bunnies—even things without eyes, like the tulip poplar seedling I rescued after it fell from a crack in the gutter where it had sprouted.

Some Americans are driven by a desire to keep a tidy

landscape or to one-up their neighbors: "yardening."
My garden's design is driven by plants, thousands of
them. The thrill for me is watching them grow, a high
surpassed only when meeting a new one that I don't
know and can grow. Television shows treat my passion
as something akin to installing Christmas lights. Put
'em up, plug 'em in, move on. I have no interest in getting
the garden "done in no time." This is something I plan
to do for the rest of my life.

In spite of the calamities that are thrown my way, I
keep coming back to the land. If a tree falls in the forest, I clean it up. I turn it into mulch or compost or into a
nurse log for azalea seeds to sprout, and I move on. I'm
part of all of this restless performance.

Why do I garden? It is a valid question. Am I crazy?
I don't really have a choice. The only way to avoid the
pangs of withdrawal from an addiction like gardening
is to garden more. This is one habit I have no intention
of breaking.

With frequent television appearances, regular articles for
the *New York Times* and most major magazines, and now his
radio show and podcast, KEN DRUSE is one of the leading
voices of natural gardening in the United States. His most
recent book is *Natural Companions*. Ken gardens in New
Jersey and in Brooklyn, New York.

Pentimento
Sydney Eddison

What could be easier or more fun for a garden writer than producing a few hundred words about the pastime that you have loved for fifty years? But I've been thinking about this question for weeks, and instead of finding it easy, I'm stumped for any single reason why I garden.

Is it because I grew up playing outside all day and loved the woods, fields, and swamps of rural Connecticut? Certainly I was captivated early on by the native flora and fauna. Or is it because my homesick English mother drew me into her world of bluebell woods and roses scrambling over ancient brick walls? She loved the gardens of home but never tried her hand at gardening here. The landscape was too rough, too unyielding, too foreign. My American father worked hard to make gardens that would please her but without the least understanding of why stiff little marigolds and tufts of purple ageratum wouldn't do the trick. He even struggled to make a "secret" garden enclosed by straggly lilacs and other common shrubs, but that didn't help either.

Thus, I was a horticultural innocent when I arrived in England to visit my mother's family in 1949. My grandmother and aunt lived in the high-walled Close of the Norwich Cathedral, with its glorious Gothic spire towering above the spikes of delphinium in Aunt Joan's garden. Then and there I fell in love with English gardens. I observed with interest my favorite aunt husbanding every spent tealeaf for her compost pile, hidden behind a bit of brick and flint wall in her tiny but beautiful garden. Aunt Joan is part of why I garden, but there's much more to it than that.

I have loved land for as long as I can remember. Growing up, I loved the shape of the hills and the craggy, wooded ridges; I loved the neighboring farmer's close-cropped cow pastures and the insignificant little stream wending its way through the mounds of moss and rushes. Swamps were my idea of paradise— so filled with gleaming marsh marigolds in the spring, and alive with small, accessible creatures like turtles and frogs. In those days, killdeer ran piping among the hummocks to lure intruders away from their nesting sites on the ground.

Many years later when my husband and I bought eight acres of old farmland a few miles from where I grew up, I felt a great stirring of familiar feelings. And so, at first, I gardened simply to be close to and part of all that I remembered and loved. I wanted to make this new piece of ground and the farmhouse resting on it, ours. I loved flowers, so I tried the plants I remembered from Aunt Joan's garden, but few survived. The roses languished and eventually died, and the delphiniums developed fungal diseases. Not forgetting my father's affection for marigolds, I planted cheerful rows of yellow 'Lemon Drop' on either side of the path up the middle of the vegetable garden.

Later, as I met other gardeners and became a better gardener myself, I began groping toward an Anglo-American style that would fit into our cow pasture without seeming out of place. Right along, I interpreted the word "garden" as the total landscape, not a series of isolated plots of vegetables or flowers. So I suppose I began gardening with some idea of the end result, but I certainly had no notion of what it would one day become. I still gardened for the fun of it and because gardening itself had begun to interest me in a new way.

Sometime after I'd gotten the hang of combining flowering plants and organizing spaces within the garden, I took classes at the New York Botanical Garden and discovered new plants and how to grow them. I'd always liked being a student, and gardening was beginning to attract me intellectually as well as emotionally. So during that phase of my life, I gardened to learn. And the more I learned, the more I realized that aspects of my former life as a drama teacher and set designer were beginning to emerge in the way I gardened.

It occurred to me that the landscape was a stage, and that a garden could function as a set with entrances, exits, and traffic patterns, a framework for action and drama. What I loved about the theater found its way into the garden. The garden also became an outlet for a love of color, painting, and art. So I think I gardened in order to feel complete. But still something was missing. I had always wanted to write. The garden gave me something to write about, and before too long, I had made a modest career of writing, speaking about gardens and gardening, and teaching other people how to do the things that I had enjoyed doing. Teaching, writing, and speaking wove together the disparate parts of my life, and it was exciting. People began to ask if they could come and see the garden, which they did in considerable numbers.

The trouble was that the garden itself had become the reason I gardened, and as the years went by, I felt less and less comfortable with that thought. The garden was never meant to be either a destination or a profession. It was something much bigger and far more important. It was the setting for a marriage that endured for forty-five years, a home to friends, students, young family members from abroad, and our beloved pets.

So once again, my reason for gardening changed.

Today, the garden is becoming simpler and its purpose clearer. I garden for the stillness of a Sunday morning when even the trucks on I-84 seem to take a break. I garden for the swish of the oscillating sprinkler and the glittering silver arcs of water wafting back and forth, the calling of birds, and the spring sun on my back. I garden for the moment.

SYDNEY EDDISON's Connecticut garden has been featured in magazines and on television. A former scene designer and drama teacher, Eddison has written seven books on gardening, lectures widely, and is a frequent contributor to *Fine Gardening* magazine and other publications. Her most recent book is *Gardening for a Lifetime*.

Turkish Delights
Fergus Garrett

I spent most of my childhood years in Turkey. Our family home, perched on a dusty hillside on the Asian side of Istanbul, overlooked the Sea of Marmara. The fields surrounding our house were gloriously littered with a profusion of wild flowers, reminding one of richly patterned Persian carpets. *Clematis viticella* smothered the hedgerows, and twiggy cistuses hugged the rocky slopes. The countryside was dotted with scrubby evergreen oaks, strawberry trees, bay laurel, and sweetly scented limes. My brother and I roamed the rolling hills, meandering streams, and sandy beaches along the coast. The outdoors became an inextricable part of our existence, forming a way of life fused with the natural world.

My grandmother was a great gardener. She was what the Turks call *eski toprak* ('old soil'), a woman close to the land. She was lean, small-framed, with striking high cheekbones and silver, slicked-back hair; her furrowed, weather-beaten skin resembled crinkled leather. Flowers were her great love and joy, and she devoted every spare moment to them, fine-tuning the paradise she had created in the small terraced garden surrounding our single storey house. Nectarines, figs, peaches, pomegranates, oranges, lemons, tangerines, cherries, quinces, apples, and pears provided the family with fresh fruit and created a gentle canopy under which my grandmother tended a lavish assortment of colourful flowers. Roses; fuchsias; pelargoniums; gladioli in the richest pinks, reds, and oranges; marigolds; Shasta daisies; and hedges of four o'clock mirabilis formed a scene that people came from miles around to see. Patches of lawn struggled in the intense Mediterranean heat while everything else flourished under her loving attention.

My grandmother allowed me to cut grass and help with watering. I loved her company, and working alongside her made me feel grown-up. Although gregarious, she seldom commented on gardening matters—no mention of scent, growing conditions, or colour. I was there to work, and work I did. I suppose it seemed incomprehensible to her that I could be interested in the subject or even one day become a gardener. With a cigarette elegantly perched between two fingers, she lost herself in her world, and I revelled in her company.

Thinking back, this early experience undoubtedly

unlocked the gardening gene that could so easily have remained latent. My grandmother didn't try to educate or inspire me by opening my eyes to the world of flowers. This came much later. But she sowed the first seeds.

For me, gardening is a complex love affair involving plants, places, and people. The brilliant Christopher Lloyd was not only a dear friend but a most generous, deeply knowledgeable, and exciting mentor—a life changer. But there have been many other, unsung heroes in my gardening life, gentle souls who have laid their hand of inspiration on me and no doubt on others like me. I garden with them all in mind, always remembering the enormous value of personal stimulation and generosity of spirit. Knowledge is not just to be accumulated but also to be passed on, and, now, from student I have graduated to teacher. But this advancement will never stop me learning; inquisitiveness—a highly desirable trait—will prevail.

Gardening engages me on many levels. Assembling plants to compose living pictures is a highly creative, multi-dimensional art form. My mother, although interested in flowers, was never a hardcore gardener, but she did have a discerning eye for colour and a profound appreciation for shape and texture. She recognised all things beautiful, and in the presence of a cultured and observant parent, we too were made aware of elegant lines, graceful porcelain, good glass, and stunningly attractive Iznik ware decorated in stylised hyacinths, tulips, and carnations. Style and creativity mattered to her, and this no doubt left a mark on my brother and me. A craving for self-expression runs deep in our family, yet for me this need is wholly satisfied by gardening, stemming any desire to write, paint, compose music, or dress in extraordinary clothes.

But gardening is not concerned solely with aesthetic expression. Other elements add to its attraction. Being closely involved with organic processes is one way of expressing my deep-felt love for the land. Gardening also speaks to my nurturing instincts; I marvel at the magic of germinating seeds and newly struck cuttings. Handling plants often reminds me of old friends and associations, or transports me to other worlds. *Verbascum olympicum* takes me two thousand metres up on the slopes of Mount Uludag in the western Pontic Alps; *Cyperus papyrus* floats me down the Nile; 'Roi des Balcons' pelargoniums set me wandering the narrow cobbled streets of Paris; *Phlomis tuberosa* lands me on the Great Hungarian Plain. Every time I encounter castor oil beans, I flip back through the pages of Ian Fleming novels; every time I prune *Rosa* 'Mrs Oakley Fisher', I think of Vita Sackville-West, who gave Christopher Lloyd a cutting many years ago. The resulting plant still thrives at Dixter and has given rise to hundreds of new progeny.

Gardening is my passion, the garden my home, and the plants my extended family. Happiness in the garden (as elsewhere in life) has required hard work and a capacity to interpret and understand the countless aspects that lead to success. Climate, changing seasons, soil, plants, the interlocking ecology of the site, sense of place, design, history, and people all play their part. In time, an innate, inbuilt sense develops that takes perception to another level. My only regret is not being able to share it with my grandmother.

FERGUS GARRETT is head gardener and CEO at Great Dixter, East Sussex, United Kingdom, where he has worked since 1992. His goal is to create stunning garden scenes year-round by combining practical skills with thorough knowledge of plants and their management. He is committed to passing on this knowledge via Great Dixter's student and volunteer program.

Paradise Regained
Nancy Goodwin

I thought I had arrived in paradise when we moved to Montrose in the late 1970s. I found good loamy soil, open sunny areas, and woodlands that had been terraced in the 1930s. Six or seven terraces followed the contours of the land and ended in a broad floodplain bordering a small river. Mature oaks and junipers dominated the skyline at the front of the property, and oaks, hickories, ashes, and maples provided shade in the surrounding woods. Areas that used to be fields had grown up with mature pines, and younger hardwoods had begun to replace these pines as they died. I believed I could grow anything here, and I knew I would never run out of space.

Three generations of Grahams, all of whom had an interest in plants, had lived on these sixty-one acres since the 1840s, so in addition to the expected native trees, we found large metasequoias, Canadian hemlocks, a pair of Nordmann firs, and several groves of mature black walnuts. The walnuts, so straight and tall, provided my first moments of disillusionment. Every acid-loving plant I brought with me from my former garden and planted in the alkaline environment of the walnuts died within the first year. Neither my father nor my husband could understand my distress at discovering that I had unsuitable conditions to grow many of my favorite plants. In fact they didn't believe it. For the first five years I failed to grow camellias, witch hazels, or rhododendrons. Even tomatoes. I finally persuaded my husband and my father that the blame lay with the walnuts and their impact on the soil, not with my incompetence. We harvested the trees near the gardens, sawed the trunks into boards and, after curing the wood for several years, turned it into stairs, shutters, a bookcase, and a table to hold the tiles from Virginia Woolf's husband's plant table.

With the walnuts gone, the gardens began to take on a new character. I grew seeds of many species of cyclamen, geraniums, dianthus, primulas, lilies, irises, and campanulas, to name a few. The old vegetable garden became a test ground for ornamental plants. I took out lawn at the front of the property and turned it into garden. Each year I explored another genus and grew as many forms and species as I could acquire. Cyclamen took on a new importance in my life. I grew and still grow every species except one, *C. somalense*—most of them throughout the woods.

Before long, deer began to appear in the new front garden each night, feasting on my choice plants. They soon brought their fawns, and I found myself unable to grow rhododendrons, camellias, witch hazels—or tomatoes—unless they were caged. The list of plants I could not grow increased with each year and finally included salvias and lantanas, which had been successful deer deterrents in the early years. I concluded that I had no choice but to erect a deer-proof fence around the entire garden. In 2008 we installed a seven-foot, nine-inch-high mesh fence around about half of our land.

"Free at last," I thought, "now I can pursue my dream." For I had cleared the weed trees off the terraced land and planted shade-loving heucheras, cyclamen, aconites, bloodroot, epimediums, and trilliums. As I began to rejoice in my new life without deer, I looked more closely and realized that, instead of fencing all the deer out, I had fenced them in. I found fresh rubbings on young trees, stumps of leaf and flower stalks where there should have been new growth or bloom, and every evening the does with their fawns returned to dine as before. I had recently read my neighbor Craig Nova's excellent novel, *The Good Son*, in which he describes a deer drive, so I asked him to help us expel these voracious creatures. We brought together about twenty-five people at dusk on our fiftieth wedding anniversary when the temperature was about a hundred degrees Fahrenheit. Craig gave us our instructions—walk slowly without talking, pause every ten steps or so, and gradually drive the deer out through the opened gates at the southwest end of the protected area. All went well until the deer panicked. About ten of them went through the gates, but the rest turned back and fled into the woods behind us. A doe hit a post and broke her neck. We were discouraged and disappointed but gathered in the shade beneath the pecan trees by the house. After waiting for the deer to recover from their trauma, we tried the walk again, this time going from west to east toward the recently opened gates on the pond side of the garden. We succeeded and drove out the remaining deer, leaving only a solitary fawn that escaped a day or so later and joined its mother on the other side of the fence. For several weeks, the deer returned. In daylight they could see the height of the fence and jumped over it; running at full speed, they broke through it. Each time they got in we drove them out, repaired the fence, and added additional netting to increase the height. Before we had finished, we could complete a successful deer drive with only three or four people. I left the cages to protect young trees for another two years, but, finally, in 2010, I concluded the deer were gone.

With the greatest excitement I watched new leaves

appear on plants I thought I had lost forever. Dianthus, daylilies, gentians, hostas, and dahlias made slow growth but enough to indicate that they were still alive. Crocuses, bloodroot, trilliums, aconites, and tiarellas produced leaves but no flowers. I planted new witch hazels, camellias, and rhododendrons, even tomatoes. Two years later these treasures and other nearly forgotten plants bloomed, and the garden exploded with flowers beyond my wildest dreams. Montrose experienced a resurrection, and I regained my paradise.

Since 1977 NANCY GOODWIN has gardened at Montrose in Hillsborough, North Carolina. She founded and managed Montrose Nursery from 1984 to 1993. She edited with Allen Lacy *A Rock Garden in the South* by Elizabeth Lawrence, wrote with Allen Lacy *A Year in Our Gardens*, and wrote *Montrose: Life in a Garden*.

Homegrown
Susan Heeger

I love our vegetable garden. Just walking around in it makes me happy—drinking in the order and action of its raised beds with their rainbow lettuce rows, curling pea vines, and kale splayed in giant topknots from knobby stems. I'm out there every morning prowling to see what's happened overnight, and soon I'm back, needing chard and collards for a breakfast shake. At noon, plants are stretching in the sun—can't miss that—and by six or seven, it's time to wander out and snip something for dinner.

Whatever else might be happening in my day, or in the world, the garden is always there, carrying on its unhurried, miraculous business in the bee-humming, earth-splitting Now. Being in it connects me to that vital present—listening, smelling, belonging to it absolutely, complete. I'm amazed how utterly it has changed my world, that I ever lived without it.

Though we already had an extensive ornamental garden around our Los Angeles house, my husband and I added the kitchen garden four years ago, when our son was a high school senior, and we began to anticipate life alone again, the two of us. The economic recession had hit, too. We saw friends losing jobs. Our own work lives were getting less predictable. We needed some all-absorbing task to perk us up, calm us down, give us a sense of our effectiveness beyond work. "Nature suffers nothing to remain in her kingdoms which cannot help itself," Ralph Waldo Emerson wrote rather sharply in his essay "Self-Reliance," and we took his words to heart.

We had both grown vegetables before, not only as a couple—in pots by the kitchen door or mixed into flower beds—but also as children, under the watchful eyes of our gardening dads. In the case of my dad, gardening was a relief and respite from jobs he hated but needed, with three children to support. Behind all our houses (and there were many, since he changed jobs often), he planted roses, camellias, whatever the garden center had on sale, and always a few rows of cucumbers, radishes, and tomatoes. We children, conscripted to help him on the weekends, glowered and complained, but we all grew up to be gardeners.

For me, that time outside sparked a complex fantasy world in which each flower and tomato was a little character, each with something to say if I would listen, something to show me about the waves of life that rose up from the earth with unstoppable determination.

So, as my husband and I eyed the sunniest spot on our city lot, the concrete-paved court where our son had played basketball and skateboarded, I felt stirred in a familiar way, excited. Rather than taking small steps that would allow us to measure our commitment, we had the concrete sawed up and relaid into four permanent, raised beds, each five feet wide and nine feet long, separated by gravel walks.

They looked huge in the beginning, filled with rich soil and tiny seedlings. But in a few months, we were greedy for more space. We ripped out a hedge along a nearby wall to gain more ground for tomatoes. We put up teepees for peas and beans and metal mesh screens where cukes and squash could climb, saving bed space for beets and more lettuce. But we let beauty have its way too, allowing dandelions to erupt in space-stealing flocks of cornflower blooms, drawing bees in droves.

We stopped going out to eat and rediscovered cooking, making soup stock from our greens and carrots, rémoulade with the root celery, caponata with the eggplant. Because our friends weren't eating out much either, it seemed friendly—and easy—to invite them over to share whatever was ready in the garden. That list grew and grew, and began to include plants we hadn't known we liked: baby turnips, kohlrabi, broccoli rabe. And since "a foolish consistency is the hobgoblin of little minds," one winter we went with 'Blauwschokker Purple' peas, the next with 'Sugar Ann' and 'Weggisser' snaps.

Very little disappointed us, as Emerson had predicted ("With the exercise of self-trust, new powers shall appear"). We discovered new skills. We became worm farmers, making super soil with their castings and stronger, more prolific plants. We learned to pair certain bed-mates and not others (beets love cabbage, straw-berries don't). We saved seeds and replanted the best of what we'd eaten—Chinese red noodle beans, Dr. Wyche's yellow and blushing pineapple tomatoes.

In the early summer, we took a tomato seedling up north to my dad. He's almost ninety, almost always in bed, and drifting in and out of the present moment. We planted the tomato near his front door, where the gardener tends and waters it. On a recent visit, when I found my dad much changed, less able even to talk to me, I noticed that the tomato was laden with fruit, still green but fat and heavy, crowding in clusters. When I told my dad, he was suddenly *right there*, in the room with me. Could I go out and take a picture?

I came back and held my digital camera so he could see the image. He smiled and squeezed my hand. He didn't have to say it: you plant the seed, you nurture it, it nurtures you. That's it. That's everything. The deepest mystery, the most irresistible thrill, just there, outside your door.

SUSAN HEEGER is a contributing editor for *Martha Stewart Living* and the Los Angeles editor-at-large for *Coastal Living*, specializing in gardening, interior design, profiles, food, and general lifestyle. She is also the co-author, with urban farmer Jimmy Williams, of *From Seed to Skillet*.

Reasonable Doubt
Daniel J. Hinkley

"Objection, your honor," the attorney protested. "The defense does not believe that the existence of a C melody saxophone in the defendant's former possession can in any way resolve the validity of the state's preposterous claim that gardening, to the accused, has somehow been simply a matter of avaricious expediency."

The judge shot a thousand-yard stare through the back of the courtroom with such force that, in a park across the street, three pigeons in a London plane fell stunned to the pavement. "Overruled," the judge intoned baldly, a sweep of silvered hair plastered flat to his scalp of murky puce. "I am vanquished by curiosity. Do go on. Puh-lease."

The prosecutor adjusted her overlarge glasses and continued her line of questioning with a self-congratulatory simper. "Mr. Hinkley, on or before your thirteenth birthday, were you or were you not given a C melody saxophone by your parents?"

"Yes," Hinkley responded, in a remarkably annoying monotone. "My dad horse-traded an old fly pole for it so I could join the school band. It looked like a standard alto sax to him."

"And did you play this instrument?" she asked, with a smile for the jury.

"I attempted to. On the first day of band that autumn, I was told that my sax was pitched in F rather than B-flat, and I had to use the score for the piccolo. But the notes for piccolos are high, screaming above the clef on ledger lines, like angry swarms of inchoate black gnats. I knew that to control the notes, I would have to know them, but my memory is not good. I could only read below the ledger lines. It was hopeless."

"Hmm," she mused, lips tightly pursed, while turning slowly toward the jury in a sinister but not ungraceful way, as kudzu might follow the sun from morning to afternoon to allow more light to fall upon its leaves. "So, regretfully, you had to abandon your dream of becoming a celebrated C melody saxophonist. And what of sports? Did you find your niche on the field?" Her high-pitched "niche" tweeted like a burst of involuntary flatulence.

"I liked sports but came to them when I was too young, and for doubtful reasons."

Her counter was immediate. "Isn't it rather true, Mr. Hinkley, that you were pathetic in every sport you tried, a downright embarrassment to a Lutheran family obsessed with Friday night lights?"

"Badgering the witness, your honor," said the defense attorney, standing abruptly. "These questions, presumably meant to imply to the jury that my client simply gardens by default, are without merit and are obviously humiliating for him to answer with honesty."

"Sustained," said the judge. "It should be perfectly apparent to the jury that this particular defendant could no more excel in sports than Sarah Palin could master critical thinking."

With a three-pointer netted and the ball in her court, the prosecutor continued. "Would it be fair to say, Mr. Hinkley, that you have found yourself to have little inherent talent for virtually everything you have tried in life?"

"At t-times it might s-s-seem so," Hinkley stuttered, like a neighbor's weedwacker burning too rich.

"And because you could find nothing else to do with any degree of success, you simply settled upon gardening, like a flip of a coin, a leap of faith, a roll of the dice, a, a—"

"Grope in the dark?" offered the judge.

"Well said, your honor," she replied.

"That's a lot of speculation," Hinkley sputtered.

"Answer the question, fat boy," said the judge.

The deflated defendant, with no answer at all, answered in the affirmative.

"And then with just a silly bit of confidence gained by germinating a maple seed, rooting some hydrangeas, and plagiarizing simplistic, anglophilic borders, you hoodwinked your contemporaries into thinking not only that you were an accomplished gardener but that you actually liked gardening."

A Perry Mason stillness filled the room. With a withering snigger, the prosecuting attorney turned to the judge. "No more questions at this time, your honor."

It was the defense attorney's turn. He rose from his seat. "Mr. Hinkley," he began (with a smile somewhat like an airport security guard who has just read your name on a boarding pass and has determined you are not going to bring down a jetliner and then tells you to have a nice day). "Do you consider yourself to be a good gardener?"

"I am a doubtful gardener with a good memory," the defendant replied.

"Objection," said Little Miss You-Know-Who. "The defendant has already testified under oath that he did not have a good memory, that he could not remember the gnat-like notes of the piccolo."

"Sustained," said the judge. "The defendant will explain the inconsistency."

"What I meant to say, is that my memory is good within the parameters of my passion," replied Hinkley.

"So you believe that you garden because you can remember?"

"I believe that to see a garden, you must first be aware of it. And to be awakened to what a garden is, in all its moments, one must remember."

"And then?"

"Like James said, my doubt is my passion and my passion is my task."

"James Dean said that?"

"Henry James."

"I knew that. Mr. Hinkley, tell the jury what else Mr. James said."

"We work in the dark, we do what we can—the rest is madness. Or words to that effect."

"Your honor, we rest our case."

DANIEL J. HINKLEY's fascination with plants goes back to his childhood in Michigan, where he studied horticulture before moving west to Washington to earn his master's degree. He writes for numerous horticultural publications and is in high demand as a speaker throughout the world. He currently gardens at Windcliff, his home in Indianola, Washington.

It All Began
with an Oxygen Mask . . .
Thomas Hobbs

'There was blood on the ceiling', my mother used to exclaim as she recounted for my five brothers and sisters the tale of my "breach-birth-by-candystriper" in a Regina, Saskatchewan, hospital. All I know is that a handy oxygen mask saved us both, and something instilled in me, at birth, a magnetic attraction to plants.

My earliest memories are not of trips to the beach, or of unwrapping Christmas presents, but rather of rummaging through neighbours' garbage looking for cast-off cut flowers. I specifically remember bringing home an exciting find of a dozen wilted red roses complete with their *Asparagus plumosa* fern filler. I was about four years old. An unknown instinct had me cut the stems into sections and try to root them in our torturous Winnipeg soil. It didn't work. By the time I entered first grade we had moved, and I was already addicted to the 'E-Z Grow' pop-up window greenhouses that cost fifty-nine cents at Woolworth's.

Nobody else in my extended family gardened, grandparents included. I do notice a recurring notation on our family tree describing a few unmarried great-uncles and great-great-uncles as 'eccentric'. This gives me hope that just maybe there is a recessive gene at work.

I now have more than fifty years of plant-associated memories to digest and analyze. One is of me, age about seven, trying to stop a crew from cutting down an ancient Russian olive (*Elaeagnus angustifolia*) with a Y-shaped trunk three or four feet in diameter. It was in the block next to our house in a pleasant Winnipeg suburb. I was sobbing. I remember my feelings of horror and anger. I was not a normal child.

Plants adopted me, I think. My parents did their best, but with six kids and their own drinking problems, I was up for grabs. Plants led me into a series of successful plant-related businesses. They steered me away from university, and wisely so. Plants decided to use me, I think. Or was it the other way round? I hope not.

If what you do for a living is also what you love, you're lucky. Gardening is a portion of what I do and what

I am, but it is part of something bigger and more all-enveloping for me. I like hybridizing plants. I started by breeding cattleya orchids. This requires a laboratory to sow the almost invisible seeds in sterile flasks of agar solution, followed by a ten-year wait to see a blossom. I still breed cymbidium orchids (but only rusts and orange tones), hemerocallis, nerines, and clivias. The reward is seeing each seedling flower for the first time. That is like Christmas morning—each new flower is different and as exciting to me as a new baby (actually, more so). Gardening has become a series of rushes—seeking a bigger high each time by creating something more beautiful than the last. I think that is why I garden. I need to create beauty. The transformation from tiny seedling, to extravagant first blossom is what propels me onward. Each charge is short-lived, so I need lots in succession. I have this all planned.

On a larger scale, I like to envision the look of a garden or garden space and work backward to make it happen. I wouldn't have a clue how to play basketball, let alone do it well. There is still a quivering bit of Janis Ian inside me, residual humiliation from Phys Ed classes. But give me three martagon lily bulbs, and I'll create a colony of dozens in just a few years—plus several hundred seedlings stashed away awaiting evaluation and a garden in which to plant them.

Joan Rivers says, 'God divides!' I think she is right.

I wouldn't trade one martagon lily for five hundred basketballs.

THOMAS HOBBS was born obsessed with plants and had his first greenhouse at age six. He runs Southlands Nursery in Vancouver, Canada, and his private garden has been featured in many prominent magazines. He gives popular lectures across North America on inspirational garden design. His most recent book is *The Jewel Box Garden*.

A Garden of Happiness
Penelope Hobhouse

The reasons for gardening change as you grow older. When I was about thirty, I had a Damascene moment. Until then I had gardened mainly to keep the weeds from coming in the door. I had visitors staying and took them to see the gardens at nearby Tintinhull House. There, the wonderful Phyllis Reiss had designed a garden of secret geometric compartments separated by yew hedges. Inside these barriers she had planted different colour schemes, using both flower and foliage to get her harmonies and contrasts. In one border she combined red, yellow, and orange flowers; in another blues and yellows, uniting the two borders with silvery-grey foliage plants. In a shady area, she used purple leaves and crimson flowers. She employed shapes and densities of trees and large shrubs to define and balance each area. In the centre of the garden, a wide canal reflected the sky. At the bottom of the garden, she grew vegetables and soft fruit in rows lined with espaliered pears, catmint, and dahlias, with views to a typical Somerset apple orchard beyond the fence. It was all spellbindingly beautiful, opening my eyes to a new world of garden possibilities.

Phyllis Reiss was gardening in what many call the 'Hidcote' or 'Sissinghurst' style but with little money and on a much-reduced scale. This made her skill in design and colour interpretation easily adaptable for modest garden areas. She had laid out the garden in the 1930s and maintained it through the war years, when getting new plants was difficult. As a result she (with one gardener) propagated many of her favourite specimens and used them in different areas for different effects. There was absolutely nothing grand about Tintinhull—it was just perfect—and it inspired me to become a real gardener.

In 1954 Phyllis Reiss gave the house and garden to the National Trust, although she continued to live at Tintinhull until her death in 1961. In 1979, more than twenty years after my first visit, I became a tenant of the Trust, looking after the house and garden and dealing with opening to the public. It was my duty to restore the garden to its appearance in Mrs Reiss's day. It was a rare privilege. By this time I had become a passionate fan of the Italian Renaissance garden, which seemed to have all the elements of classical design. As I wrote books and sketched plans for clients, Tintinhull and the quieter tones of Italy remained my inspiration. I loved the concept of perfect proportions and compartments that provided the opportunity to try out different schemes, some full of bright colours, others mainly green, with peaceful grey stone and evergreens. My designs often echoed the same theme: a strong structured layout, inside which I could create a contrived jungle or manicured flowerbeds to suit a site or my clients. I believed, as I still do, that to garden is to produce order out of nature's chaos.

There was another aspect of gardening at Tintinhull that appealed: we produced all our own annuals from seed and regularly propagated any old or tender shrubs. This taught me a valuable lesson. Gardening is not about instant gratification. It is a process—from seedling to flower (a matter of a few weeks) and from small rooted cutting to a useful shrub (often a few years). This whole process, rather than the ultimate product, seems to me half the joy of gardening. At first when I was designing, particularly in the United States, I had a problem persuading new gardeners that a true garden devotee would be happy to wait. Now in my eighties I enjoy propagating almost more than any other garden activity. I like the anticipation and am always happiest when working alone.

The fourteen years I spent at Tintinhull must have been a preparation for another stage in my gardening development. After studying Italian garden history, I moved on to the gardens of Islam and became more aware of the spiritual element of gardening. Islamic gardens are always simple, reflecting their desert origins: vertical cypresses, fruit trees, water rills with the sound of trickling fountains, and quiet places to sit and meditate. Today I see my own garden as a refuge, a sanctuary, an enclosure, and an escape from ordinary life. It is up to me to make it as near to Paradise as possible. I am not a Muslim, but if there is a heaven, I believe it will be a beautiful garden. Of course, I also cheat quite a lot about my garden's design quality; it is very personal. I love unusual and tender plants, and any success I have with them makes me happy. Each morning brings new shoots to cherish. Perhaps I should use 'happiness' rather than 'spirituality' as my true reason for gardening.

PENELOPE HOBHOUSE is a garden writer, designer, and historian. For fourteen years until 1993 with her husband, Professor John Malins, she was in charge of the National Trust Gardens at Tintinhull House in Somerset, England. She lives in Dorset and travels in Europe, central Asia and India, and the United States, lecturing and designing gardens.

A Rocky Start
Panayoti Kelaidis

When I was eight, my beautiful sister Mary (eighteen years my senior) married Allan, and for a while they lived in our house with my extended big, fat, Greek family. Unlike my short, aged, foreign-born parents (with accents and opinions to match), Allan was an Anglo—tall and incredibly cool. He soon began to build a rock garden along the north side of our house, spending every day outside on the project. Could I be blamed for wanting to help him at every stage of the process? In retrospect, I realize that I was an alibi as well as a nuisance: "Allan's out there with the kid." Ergo, it's OK that he's not in the noisy household. I shadowed him through the entire enterprise, talking more or less nonstop. I accompanied him on a dozen or more drives up Sunshine and Boulder Canyons to scrounge the roadside granite boulders that comprise the garden to this day. Most were large, one-man rocks (100 pounds more or less) and all must have been a chore to load. An eight-year-old isn't exactly helpful in such enterprises. But I was company.

It is hard to imagine today (the rock garden is still there, shrouded with weeds) how raw it must have looked at first. The rounded, gray Precambrian granite boulders were harsh. Now they're encrusted with lichens. We borrowed my father's truck and brought down yards and yards of decomposed granite for fill. I would watch Allan wrestle and fuss and place rocks for hours and hours. I remember asking a lot of questions. The answers to the questions sometimes sounded just a tad perfunctory. An older or wiser child would have known I was driving him nuts—a strange Greek chorus to the drama of the garden's creation. It wasn't grand—some eight feet wide at most, tapering to a mere four feet at the east end, and some forty-five feet long, but I remember that it seemed to take forever to finish. I thought it was the most wonderful thing in the world.

I blush to say we stole many of the original plants. Back then it wasn't exactly larceny: everyone thought it was perfectly fine to dig up plants in the wild. It was definitely not acceptable to filch bits from private gardens, however, but we frequently did. The principal source of new plants was a garden a block and a half away on Fourteenth Street. Namely, Paul and Mary Maslin's garden. Allan stuck to sedums and sempervivums, which are admittedly extremely portable. I was excruciatingly self-conscious as we loped ever so casually along the front of the Maslin garden, pausing innocently enough, leaning down and then I'd see Allan was breaking off bits here and there and stuffing them in his pocket. Years later, after I became best friends with Paul, he was dumbfounded when I confessed what we'd done. He never trusted me wholly thereafter. I'm a more honest adult as a consequence.

Allan and I also visited Nuzum's Nursery, over on Boulder Creek. It tumbled down a steep hill at several levels. There we purchased *Campanula garganica*, which persisted in the same spot for the better part of a half-century, blooming magnificently every spring.

The real glories of the garden, however, were a handful of aubrietas that grew rapidly to form large mats, knitting the granite boulders together with trim, hairy, dark blue-green rosettes. Starting in April, these would be smothered for weeks on end with shimmering deep purple rose, or refulgent blue cruciform flowers of a furious hue. To this day, when I see aubrietas I magically shrink in age to the single digits.

Then one day Allan and Mary moved away, to Berkeley, for graduate school. In the bustle of family parting, Allan pulled me aside. The responsibility of the rock garden rested upon my shoulders now, he told me. I had to take care of it for him. He would come back some day and see how I fulfilled my duties, or words to that effect. I remember wincing inwardly: could I do it? Fortunately, he had left a whole shelf of gardening books behind, including brand-new rock garden books by Kolaga and Foster that would be my bedtime reading for months and years to come. I almost memorized them.

Somewhere in my papers I still have some of the early plant orders I made when I realized that I needed to add many more "choice" plants to the still sparse garden. My favorite catalogue was from Lounsberry Gardens, in Illinois. I remember the color pictures (which stayed distressingly the same year after year) of eastern and midwestern wildflowers.

There is a special smell that well-packed flowers have when they have been properly shipped through the mail: a fragrant moistness as you unwind the newspaper and sphagnum, or (not as much fun) the plastic wrap and rubber bands. Foliage and sometimes flowers have been bruised a bit but often seem to expand under your gaze, relieved to have a little fresh air. You gather them into a waterproof flat, and give them a gentle mist and put them in a cool, well-ventilated spot to harden off. Some may take a few weeks to acclimate; some you must pot up. Often in a few days you can start to find places to plant the toughies in the garden. Mail-order gardening is one of the greatest and least-sung pleasures available to humankind.

In these days of ready travel it is hard to believe that several summers elapsed before Allan and Mary returned to Boulder. It was relatively late in the day when their car drove up, and I remembered how excited I was to show off the vastly improved rock garden, filled with no end of interesting new plants I'd managed to purchase and collect.

To my consternation, Allan and Mary seemed primarily absorbed by my parents and extended family. One of them patted me on the head (my, how I'd grown), but I couldn't quite find the moment to push the issue of the garden. After all, Allan had told me how important it was. Why was he procrastinating?

Inside there was food and commotion, and I kept sidling up to Allan, trying to catch his eye, waiting for him to look at me knowingly and say, "Let's go check out that garden." I noticed with a shock that it was getting dark outside. I screwed my courage to the sticking-place and forced myself to ask, rather sheepishly, "Allan, don't you want to go out and see the garden?"

The pause was interminable.

"What garden?"

"The rock garden."

"Oh, we'll have time to see that tomorrow morning."

To paraphrase Nabokov, a turret collapsed on a distant castle.

Anyone who remembers childhood can imagine that this was a defining moment for me. In one instant I realized that, although I would love Allan anyway, unconditionally and forever, I would never again experience such a pang of ridiculous disappointment. From that moment on the garden was entirely mine. And unbeknown to me, my career path and future began to quietly assemble from the shattered illusions.

PANAYOTI KELAIDIS is a plant explorer, gardener, and administrator at Denver Botanic Gardens, where he is now senior curator and director of outreach. He began his career at the garden as curator of the rock alpine garden, where he designed and oversaw the initial plantings. He is responsible for introducing most of the hardy South African succulents currently in cultivation.

Foreign Relations
Roy Lancaster

I am a professional gardener, but that was not my original plan. I was always passionate about wildlife and wild country, but at age fifteen my mind was set on driving a steam engine on the railways. Fortunately the wildlife won, thanks to the advice of a museum curator, my first guru, who persuaded me to interview for a job with my local parks department. That was in 1952.

Once at work, two parks foremen took me in hand, introducing me to the botanical names of plants and stories of their origins, as well as the more practical matters of growing and using them. It wasn't the last time I benefitted from others' experience, and of course I still do.

Much as I enjoyed growing plants and gardening, it was the images of plants in their native lands and tales of the people associated with their discovery and introduction into cultivation that fuelled my imagination.

Since school days, I had pursued an interest in my native flora and that, in some respects, prepared me for the bigger picture. In 1971, when I was invited to join a plant hunting expedition to East Nepal, I had no hesitation in accepting.

My Nepal experience was the first of many such travels, and apart from the sheer adventure of it all, my experiences and observations taught me how better to understand why plants choose to grow where they do, which had important repercussions for me as a gardener. This brings me to the nub of why I garden.

Let me start in the present, in my suburban garden of one-third of an acre located between Winchester, England's ancient capital, and the port city of Southampton. My wife Sue and I chose the house, a late Victorian building, in 1982, when our second child was expected. The smaller front garden to the north of the house is situated on the Bracklesham Beds, a well-drained acidic sand above gravel, which I tell visitors is the nearest we have in England to the Gobi Desert. To the rear of the house lies a heavier, clay soil. On two sides we are bounded by neighbour's hedges, mostly cherry laurel, *Prunus laurocerasus*, which conceals old tree stumps, long time sources of honey fungus, *Armillaria mellea*.

This isn't my first garden, but it is probably my last, and it contains many of the ingredients I find most agreeable and exciting in the plant world. First is the geographical representation. I can look through our windows or stroll around the garden and see plant representatives of countries from around the temperate world, many of which I have visited. In one small border alone I can enjoy *Grevillea victoriae* (S.E. Australia), *Calceolaria pavonii* (Peru), *Hedychium ×moorei* 'Tara' (Nepal), *Cobaea pringlei* (Mexico), *Deutzia multiradiata* (China), and *Eucomis montana* (S. Africa). I tell myself that in my dotage these plants will trigger memories of long-ago adventures, or else remind me of countries I have never visited. I find that in looking at plants I have seen in the wild—a Japanese maple from the woodlands of Honshu, red-flowered *Lobelia tupa* from the shores of Chile, the shrubby dwarf oak *Quercus sadleriana* from the Siskiyou Mountains of S.W. Oregon—I can conjure up scenes of those places, whence they originated.

Just as important to me are the memories spurred by plants in my garden. *Bergenia purpurascens* 'Len Beer', for example, recalls my dear friend and leader of the Nepal expedition, who died in 1977; and the giant honeysuckle *Lonicera calcarata*, now growing on the south wall of our house, brings to mind Japanese botanist Mikinori Ogisu, who introduced the plant from Emei Shan, China. If all the individuals who have generously given me plants were to attend my garden for a reunion, the queue would stretch down the road, while the spirits of those no longer here would crowd the trees above, and, oh, the tales they would tell.

We plantsmen are sometimes dismissed as mere collectors, and while I admit to maintaining a goodly collection of trees, shrubs, climbers, and perennials from the ornamental to the curious, I can justify it on the grounds that as a communicator it helps enormously to have these plants, each with its own story, under my nose where I can observe them at all times of the day and night. To see moonlight washing the pale stems of *Eucalyptus pauciflora* subsp. *debeuzevillei*, a snow gum, is an experience to savour.

In the early years, I was hesitant about inviting those with a keen eye for design to visit my garden, believing that the plants were more important to me than the landscape, but encouraged by my wife Sue's observations I believe the plants now look comfortable in a setting that allows them to make the most of their individual merits.

Writing these words in my garden on a sunny late afternoon in August, with the scent of *Lilium* 'Casablanca' hanging in the air, the sound of doves filtering from a *Magnolia cylindrica* heavy with red fruits, and the sight of hoverflies on a nectar-rich sedum, I feel a sense of achievement and of calm as well as an acceptance that there is still more to come. The most important reason I garden must be the therapeutic benefits it provides. I have only to rise from my bed in the morning, draw back the curtains and see the garden below, its plants assembled like performers on a stage, to feel refreshed and raring to go. Whatever the season, come rain or shine, there is always a plant, at least one, about to put on a show.

Plantsman, writer, lecturer, and broadcaster ROY LANCASTER has travelled all over the world on plant exploration trips, including expeditions to Nepal and China. He is president of the Hardy Plant Society and a vice president of the Royal Horticultural Society, for whose journal, *The Garden*, he writes a regular column. He lives in Hampshire, England.

Family Dynamics
Tovah Martin

To set the record straight, I don't garden of my own free will. I am held hostage. Always have been.

Not long after birth, some green thing or other (the memory is blurred) grabbed me. No struggle ensued, just complete and total submission. I joined the ranks.

Before I could even walk, I was crawling into the garden, I guess. As a child I monopolized sweater drawers for storing marigold seeds. Other little girls yearned for ballet slippers, while I clomped around in work boots. Adults baited me to name a future career choice: "What do you want to be when you grow up, little girl?" I didn't have to think twice. I wanted to be a butterfly.

When I went to work at Logee's Greenhouses, the world shrank around me. There was nothing beyond the splash of hoses, the hum of fans, the vines snarling my hair, and the thwack of a bird throwing itself against the greenhouse glass in a desperate effort to get free after it had squeezed through the vents. I was definitely not that bird.

I arrived in winter—temporarily, I thought—and took an upstairs bedroom in the little house beside the greenhouses. After dark, I could look down on the glass houses with their lights illuminating the plants and survey the green world within. I would watch the tropical plants, crawling around walls and walkways. I had a bird's eye view of the passionflowers, bent on holding the world in their tendrils, and the eighty-year-old Ponderosa lemon bearing its weighty fruit. That's what clinched the deal, really—watching the tropicals all going crazy, groping and growing, sending their exotic roots down deep into the rich, brown New England soil beneath the greenhouse floor. Half the night, I would marvel at that contained world of tropical green, dappled in blossoms from the far reaches of the world, counterpoised against the howling winds and bitter temperatures of Connecticut. By daylight, I trotted the greenhouse aisles, pushing my way through the undergrowth, ducking below the overgrowth to tend the plants. Of course, it wasn't all acceptance and "thank you, ma'am." I pruned back the rampant bougainvilleas and received only scratches for thanks.

Logee's hired me for my height, of that I am sure. Only I could fit into the sunken herb pit without smacking my head on the entrance beam. I could squeeze beneath the *Jasminum rex* and around the *Alstroemeria pulchella*. That was part of my job description. The plants had seniority. I answered to the allamanda. I ran out in thunderstorms to crank down the manual vents when rain threatened to drown a succulent. I dragged plants (thousands and thousands of plants) into safe havens in advance of hurricanes that might flatten them. And I wept a river when my favorite topiary lantana snapped in two. It didn't feel like either heroics or histrionics at the time. The point is that the collection was paramount. The plants were family.

At some point, I shifted my focus outside the glass and began shoving plants into the ground. Initially, it was just an exercise in seeing what the tropicals would do in open air ("Be free, *Mandevilla boliviensis*"), but later my focus strayed, into perennial borders and shrubberies.

And I moved on from Logee's. Now I live in my own little cottage with perennials, tropicals, herbs, and vegetables scattered pretty much everywhere. Gardens surround the house, and houseplants pack the windowsills. It is my house, but the plants still reign. If a viburnum pops up like a cowlick smack dab in the middle of a garden, well, that's where it remains. I celebrate its radiant health and welcome compliments on its overachievement. Not only don't I inflict a whole lot of design dictums on my plants, but I take offense when anyone offers a reality check. I always say that love is blind. You laugh, but it's true.

I walk the meadow and imagine that the goldenrod gives me the glad hand as I pass by. The space could have been a pool area, I suppose. Perhaps a tennis court. But that wouldn't be me. Or, us. But don't take this too far. When the goldenrod encroaches on the blueberries, it's curtains. I'm idealistic, but there are limits.

I read somewhere that any self-respecting garden should have a "program." Meaning it should serve a function in your life. Really? The concept honestly never occurred to me. It's nice that the pine wrestles the winds before those gusts plow into the house. But I didn't bring it onto the property demanding that it perform that job for me. I planted it because it called to me at the nursery. Then I tucked it into place.

Basically, I'm still bending myself to accommodate the botanicals in my life. Yes, membership in the knee-cracking, back-groaning society of gardeners has rewards—the first bulbs of spring, the fragrances that float on a slight breeze, and the freshly opened flower—but I don't see this relationship as reciprocal. I know who's boss. I wish I could say that I garden for the joggers who sputter and groan their way down Main Street. But that's not why I garden. I garden for them—for all those green things that roped me into servitude years ago. I like to think they need me.

An avid (verging on obsessed) gardener, indoors and out, TOVAH MARTIN has worked her way through the gardening gamut. Her areas of specialty include bulbs, heirloom gardening, terrariums, houseplants, tropicals, exotics (especially begonias), cottage gardening, and horticultural therapy. Through writing she shares the contagion from her Connecticut garden.

The Dirty-Minded Gardener
Julie Moir Messervy

My favorite *New Yorker* cartoon depicts an overlook to a distant mountainscape, a truck with "Joe's Landscaping" painted on it, and two men in work clothes surveying the view. The caption reads, "I would have done this differently."

That could have been me talking. I see the world as a garden, finding beauty at every turn, but I also feel the need to tweak the location of nearly every tree, shrub, focal point, or bed line I've ever seen. Move it a bit to the left! Line things up! Prune out the deadwood! If you looked at a landscape through my eyes, you'd always find a way to alter things so that the whole looked even more perfect. That seems to be the essence of why I garden.

For I'm a mind gardener—I design landscapes in my

mind's eye. When I visit a new client's property, I see a hundred ways to integrate inside with outside, make it flow, play up the focal points, or craft the details. My problem is not in coming up with ideas, it's usually in overwhelming clients with possibilities. As I wrote in *The Inward Garden* (1995):

> If you are a pure mind gardener, you may be perfectly content to never actually finish planting your garden, because you can so vividly imagine what it will become. For you, every undug hole is filled with exotic species, each unsightly view soars as a distant vista. You may not require an actual garden because you already have a fully developed paradise in your soul.

From earliest childhood I was a mind gardener, making gardens out of the landscapes around me—little hidey-holes and miniature rooms of moss, pine needles, acorns, sticks, and stones. While I always loved dolls' houses, I preferred to arrange the tiny furniture without benefit of walls, so I could envision living wherever— and however—I wanted. Growing up in the suburbs in an energetic seven-kid family, I sought out contemplative places in nature, sprucing up the forests, fields, and orchards around me so they felt like home.

My mother, by contrast, was always a dirt gardener. She loved nothing more than being in her garden, staking, dividing, mulching, and moving her plants around. When I was young, we lived on the North Shore of Chicago, where she tended an elaborate vegetable garden, complete with Concord grapes that we'd eat off the vines, puckering up and spitting the skins at each other. She also created borders of bearded iris, pinks, and snapdragons whose heads we'd pluck and converse with on the lawn. As I wrote,

> If you are a dirt gardener, you are a gardener of the hands; a fierce worker who devotes many a waking moment to the quest for the exact spot to put a favorite delphinium or the best organic deterrent for the Japanese beetle. You feel most comfortable contemplating your garden world close-up—down to the petals, the stamen, and the worms. . . . You are a gardener who uses an ornamental bench to stack pots or display annuals rather than—heaven forbid—as a seat.

When I was eleven, we decamped to Connecticut—to a beautiful pink house with a hillside of terraced gardens and an Italian gardener. After a month of Giuseppe's services, my parents dispensed with him and put the kids to work. We spent entire Saturdays boxing boxwoods and raking leaves. But there was also time for lolling with friends on the beautifully constructed stone terraces. It was a romantic place for an adolescent girl to grow up in; the house had a Romeo and Juliet balcony, sleeping porches, and a tiny hidden door I once found in a closet with just a pile of soot inside. That garden taught me the importance of flow, with the low curving bluestone steps that moved one gracefully from one grassy level to another; and of differentiating experiences in a garden. Our round and shady "Black Terrace" (so called because of the color of our wrought iron furniture) was situated under a massive maple tree; it had a completely different atmosphere from that of our sunny rectangular "White Terrace," which formed the space between the living room and the two wings of the house.

My budding design sensibilities were honed in college, where I majored in art history, and later did a master's degree in both architecture and city planning. Halfway into my graduate studies, I opened a book on Japanese garden design and felt as though I had come home, back to my childhood daydreaming places. To discover that someone could have a career making places of beauty and meaning was life-changing. I arranged to study and live in Kyoto, working for a garden master and learning the art of garden-making, Japanese style.

Under Kinsaku Nakane's tutelage, I learned many practical things such as how to pluck pines, prune azaleas, and pound moss into place. But his most valuable advice was to take time to visit as many gardens

as possible, studying first-hand the deep garden tra-
dition in over eighty landscapes in Kyoto and around
the country.

Upon my return to the United States, I finished graduate school and started building gardens and teaching
about my Japanese experience. I married, had three
children, and continued designing, teaching, and writing about landscape design theory and practice as my
understanding of the field grew.

Fast forward thirty-five years—six books, untold
numbers of lectures, scores of design projects. Now, in
the last third of my life, what fascinates me is starting
to change. Indeed, personality theory holds that in mid-
life and beyond, we "try out" the non-preferred parts of
our temperament. It seems that I'm becoming a dirt gardener at last. Here's what has happened:

I moved to the country—and so was brought full circle to my childhood roots. Only now it's not just play.
I'm also responsible for stewarding the natural world
around me. Not only do my husband and I carry on a
continuous battle with buckthorn and other invasives
on our property in southern Vermont, but I also tend a
big vegetable garden, orchards, and extensive perennial
gardens, for which I'm the sole proprietor. I'm learning
the craft of gardening from the ground up.

The landscape design studio I run is full of young
and talented women who know anything I don't about

gardening. Together, we continue to design landscapes for residential, institutional, and public clients. My life as a designer is no longer just about me—it's about us and I love it this way. Read our blog and you'll see.

As an educator and writer, I've moved from a more conceptual approach to gardening (*Contemplative Gardens*, *The Inward Garden*, *The Magic Land*) to a more pragmatic explication of garden theory for homeowners (*Outside the Not So Big House, Home Outside*). It's one of several ways I'm trying to help the average person to get outside into their own backyard again. I created our new online design service and iPhone/iPad landscape design app, to give everyone a chance to dream up and build their home outside.

I am part of a new wave of homesteaders who are growing their own vegetables, raising chickens, bees, and livestock, and living on the land as lightly as possible. I am mindful of behavioral ecologist Doug Tallamy's research into native plants, showing how our headlong rush to develop nature has resulted in sterilized environments that are destroying the biodiversity that insects, birds, and all other animals need to survive. His work is fundamentally altering the way I now think about what I should be doing as a landscape designer.

Yet, like Joe the landscaper, I still believe I can make the world more beautiful by creating the elegant bed line, balancing the colors in a mass planting, or finding that dynamic focal point. What I've become is a hybrid of both mind and dirt gardeners—a dirty-minded gardener! Despite the heat, ticks, deerflies, mosquitoes, and backbreaking work, I can't think of anything else I'd rather be.

With three decades of experience, JULIE MOIR MESSERVY has emerged as a leader of a movement in which landscape design is as much a personal journey as it is about leaving a unique imprint upon the earth. Her most recent books are *Home Outside: Creating the Landscape You Love* and *The Toronto Music Garden*. She lives and gardens in southern Vermont.

The Flower Thief
Stephen Orr

I had a youthful predilection for larceny. It doesn't affect me much these days, but I must admit that under certain circumstances and in certain gardens, the temptation returns. My problem started early, as a preteen. It was not the daring, shoplifting sort of thievery that I heard about from the cool kids in school; it was something quieter and gentler. I was an unapologetic plant swiper. Specifically, I was compelled to steal any attractive flower that caught my eye in a neighbor's front yard.

Why did I do it? I, like most anyone else, appreciate the beauty of a flower, and, of course, I knew my actions were wrong. My parents told me so in no uncertain terms the few times they caught me red-handed with loot or discovered one of my flowery treasure troves. But my youthful self could never enjoy a perfect blossom at a distance, growing on someone else's bush; I had to possess and sequester it away only for myself. I would case neighborhood gardens in my West Texas town, watching to see when a certain 'Betty Prior' rose would be at its peak or a row of pyracantha berries was about to ripen. Then, under cover of night or even early morning, I would strike—a five-year-old armed with scissors and a shoebox, ducking through shadowy foundation plantings to avoid passing headlights. Snipping away here and there like a mad barber, I would help myself. Then I would sneak back home to arrange the plant snippets in one of my favorite hiding places: a hidden corner behind the woodpile, my bedroom closet, or most often, our dog Chester's unused doghouse, which I could just barely squeeze into.

I remember this last stashing spot most of all. I used it for a few months until the day my father discovered its hiding-in-plain-sight location. I can only imagine his bewilderment as he looked inside the small opening to see my macabre shrine to Flora. I would visit my collection from time to time as if stopping in a museum, viewing the carefully arranged flowers, berries, and vines that looped around nails in the unpainted plywood walls—all dried in the Texas summer heat. My dad would have known immediately that we didn't grow most of the floral offerings in this ersatz temple. When he sternly questioned me, like a young George Washington I didn't dare to lie or even deny that the plants had arrived at our home from sources outside our own property. I don't recall the punishment he gave me at the time (sorry, Dad)—maybe because I knew in my heart of hearts that I would be a repeat offender.

I do remember the outcome of another case. My mother found a large stash of fresh scarlet nandina berries in my closet one morning. Within five minutes, I was standing at Mrs. Ramsey's front door, in tears, handing her a box of her now useless berries while my mother stood angrily at the curb. The embarrassment of this punishment did the trick, in a way. I became even more stealthy. I made sure never to pick too many of any one plant, nor did I make the mistake of using such an obvious hiding place. My crime wave continued on a smaller, more surreptitious scale for a few more summers, until one day I grew out of my plant-stealing stage. Maybe I finally realized the negative moral implications of helping myself to someone else's property without permission, or perhaps I realized the embarrassment I would suffer having to greet Mrs. Ramsey again with a box of berries as a junior high schooler. I knew if I kept up such activities as a young adult, word would get around—and quickly.

I tell you this, not merely as a childhood confession but to describe one of the main reasons that I love making gardens as an adult. There is so much beauty out in the natural world, and through the act (and art) of gardening, I can summon it, possess it, and even sequester it in my garden. But more often these days, I choose to share the things that I grow with my friends, neighbors, and the people who read the articles and books that I write. Maybe I'm making amends to the sweet elderly gardeners in Abilene who felt the disappointment of having their delicate blue anemones plundered in a pre-dawn raid all those years ago. Or maybe it's the straight-forward happiness I see in others and myself when I bake a chicken with handfuls of just-picked herbs. Or the satisfying feeling when a neighbor stops by the front garden of my co-op apartment building in the city and remarks that she goes out of her way to pass our side-walk plantings each day with her daughter on their walk to school so they can see what is coming up. I don't even mind so much when I see that a half-sized pass-erby has chopped the head off a tulip that dared stick its head outside the wrought iron garden fence. I can eas-ily identify where that childish and ultimately selfish thought process originates. Who knows? Maybe some-day that same little flower thief will grow up to make horticulture his or her profession, spreading the joy of gardening through words and actions to a wide audi-ence. And to think all that might begin with someone's irresistible urge to snatch a bit of passing beauty.

STEPHEN ORR shares his love of horticulture as the editorial director for gardening at *Martha Stewart Living*. Pre-viously, Orr was the garden editor at both *House & Garden* and *Domino* magazines. In addition he has written for the *New York Times*, the *Wall Street Journal*, and other publica-tions. He is the author of *Tomorrow's Garden*.

Value Added
Anna Pavord

The point of my garden is to increase the value of my life. My garden locks me into the slow inevitable rolling out of the seasons, cycles of growth and decay, the lengthening of days and the shortening of shadows—a world that cities make us forget.

My garden not only gives me pleasure, it also instils calm, grafts patience into my soul. Gardening slows me down and puts worries in proportion. My garden teaches me to be observant and how to look at things. I become less inclined to leap to conclusions or jump onto the latest bandwagon. A garden hones my senses. I can hear the sound of dampness creaking through the soil and smell it hovering in different guises over the compost heap. In a garden, I never feel lonely.

Nor do I ever feel bored. Though constant in the sense that it is rooted in one particular place (and thereby roots me), a garden is deliciously inconstant in its particulars. The light falls on a garden and reflects from it in a different way every day. Breezes move through it from different directions. Trees provide different silhouettes at different times of the year. The arrival and disappearance of seasonal plants happens almost faster than I can keep up with. And this is all free. You don't need wads of money to garden.

At the heart of the whole business is the feeling that, when we garden, we abandon a timetable constructed around dentist's appointments, car services, and the possible arrival of trains, to plunge headlong into a completely different timetable, an immense and inexorable one entirely outside our control.

This, of course, is not a conscious feeling. When I wander out the back door to do some casual gardening I do not say, "Fancy that. I am part of the great diurnal round." I just get on with the weeding. But while I am there, idly looking at the silhouette of ferns in the dusk, and the sun sets around me, bleeding across the sky with that savage intensity that makes the hair stand up on the back of my neck, I feel a whole lot better than I do indoors.

This feeling is, to a certain extent, satisfied by a good long country walk. The extra dimension gardening adds is that we are actively involved in the process; inherent in the whole business of making a garden is the creation of a setting. A gardener makes a sort of dream, a world in his own image or a world to blot out the image of the real one that lies outside his boundaries.

Knitted into the process of making, of creating, is a sense of escape. In my garden I can fashion the kind of world I want to live in. Some gardeners are control freaks. Edging and cutting back and tying in are always to the forefront of their minds. Others drift through a blur of foxglove and wild briar that would drive control freaks round the bend. Some are unsure who they are and so hire landscape designers to tell them.

The act of creating a garden gives me the pleasure of *making* something, of feeling that my labour alone has transformed an eight-foot square of concrete into a place that delights. As far as I'm concerned, creating a garden is as valid an artistic experience as anything that Rodin may have felt, bashing away at his stone. We cannot all sculpt. We cannot all paint or make music. But we can all learn to garden.

"The first purpose of a garden is to be a place of quiet beauty such as will give delight to the eye and repose and refreshment to the mind," said the plantswoman Gertrude Jekyll in *A Gardener's Testament*. She wrote that towards the end of her life, and it sums up exactly what I feel. A good garden delights more senses than any other art. You can smell it, touch it, listen to it, look at it, eat it. Eating it was important when we had children at home. Now, less so.

What I want now is to feel that when I step into my garden I am entering a different world, one that has nothing to do with anger, frustration, or sorrow. As a Hindu leaves his shoes at the entrance to the temple, so I can temporarily cast off life's grubbier aspects and float. Tranquillity.

What enhances this tranquillity? Sometimes it is the delicious sense of profusion that comes from plants growing in places that suit them. I like a slight sense of order too, for it is this that separates gardens from what lies over the wall. Order does not necessarily infer tidiness or lack of weeds. It implies a comfortableness with the way that things are disposed around you, a natural inevitability in the lines that the paths take, a design that is not so much imposed on as released from the site.

And in the present financial climate, we gardeners are in a very fortunate position. The value of our patches—the real value, I mean, not some price-per-square-foot dreamed up by a wonky estate agent—doesn't zoom up and down because of events out of our control. Its pleasures don't diminish because the stock market is dropping like lead. The plant for which you paid £2.50 yesterday is still worth that today (in fact it is surely worth three times that—the cheapness of plants is among life's great mysteries).

One of the best tricks a garden plays is that you never quite remember how it's going to be, that first day after winter has gone, when you go outside and can stay outside all day fiddling with jobs that aren't pressing enough to weigh heavily but will nevertheless pay dividends. A garden is made up of a thousand small interventions, but each small act is a defence (defiance even) against a world without anchors or safe harbours.

ANNA PAVORD is the gardening correspondent for the *Independent* and the author of nine books, including the bestselling *The Tulip*. She contributes to a number of magazines, both in the United States and the United Kingdom, and regularly fronts programs for BBC Radio 3 and 4. Her most recent book is *The Curious Gardener*. She lives in Dorset, England.

The Accompanist
Anne Raver

I garden for many reasons other than growing the thing itself, though watching a tree or a tomato or a poppy grow is a slow, deep joy.

But I'm not focused so much on the goal—the bountiful harvest, the exquisite design, the perfectly pruned roses. The gardens on this old farm in central Maryland, planted around the clapboard house by my grandparents and my parents, are never pruned at the right time. The old privet hedge gets shaggy and blooms, gloriously, because there's always something more pressing, or interesting, than shearing the monster that grows, no matter how neglected, alongside the road.

Perhaps I garden for all that accompanies the act of gardening: the nutty-sweet fragrance of black locust blossoms, on a rainy afternoon in May, when the silver-gray clouds make the trees look like gray-green ghosts, laden with white blossoms; the flash of a sky-blue wing, as a bluebird flies from its nest in the hollow of a tree, and swoops, in that particular bluebird way, over the field where I'm planting my tomatoes.

I love the physicality of gardening, my knees in the dirt, my bare hand wielding a trowel to dig a little trench in this Maryland clay, lightened by years of our compost and the manure of my neighbor's cows. I lay my Brandywines horizontally, covering them up, as children do to each other at the beach, right up to their necks in the warm sand. Only this is warm, silty loam, which seduces me to take off the gloves I know I should wear but rarely do.

I started these tomatoes with seed saved at the end of last summer—of some bulbous, orange-red beauty whose sweet-acid flavor I can almost taste again, if I close my eyes. I raised them in our greenhouse, a home-made contraption built with friends one winter on the side of a shed that once housed pigs. These seedlings, so robust and green by mid-May, which is their usual planting time, grew leggy and pale waiting out the seemingly endless cold, rainy nights of last spring.

Finally, I got them in the ground, and in their mirac-ulous way, they began to green up and leaf out, within days. (This is part of why I garden, witnessing this resilience.)

"Tomatoes are weeds," my favorite extension agent says. "You can't kill them if you try."

A good plant for a gardener like me.

Maybe I most love what I call the un-garden. The wildlings that grow up, when you don't weed or mow. The scarlet and purple poppies (*Papaver somniferum*) bobbing their fragile petals in the garlic patch, the lusty sunflowers towering over certain crops, like my bush beans (haricots verts, picked when thinner than pencils) and cukes (little crunchy Kirbys, for pickling).

When I failed to prune the privet, it kept growing taller (twelve feet as I write and heading skyward) and wider (five feet, by now, at least) and bloomed in early June with thousands of white spires that filled the air with the heady scent of pistachio ice cream.

We've let my grandfather's boxwood along the walk to the front porch go, too. The clipped orbs he once pruned have grown into great rumpled mounds, a good ten feet over our heads, inspired by the collection at the U.S. National Arboretum, which are never sheared.

We stopped mowing so much around the old farmstead, which has been in my family since 1795; now, in place of cropped lawn, tall grasses and ox-eye daisies sway on the slope that runs up to the front of our bank barn. Rock, my partner (is there no good word for a sixty-something boyfriend?), mowed a wide path to the front door of what is now our home—two floors of airy, wide-open spaces, with a wall of south-facing windows lighting the loft where I once built tunnels in the hay.

We garden now, in the old walled barnyard and in a field beyond its curving stone wall.

I grew up on this place, never thinking I would return for anything other than Christmas and funerals. But then the years went by, of living in cities and watery places of great beauty, of traveling through jungles and great gardens, of walking across deserts and trash lots turned into gardens. And, eventually, I came back to these rolling hills.

Now, in this steamy climate, where summers are hotter than I ever remember, where weeds grow faster and taller on the CO_2 we humans pour into the air (which is why I leave the yard unmown, and rake my leaves, and hang my clothes out to dry), I am astounded by the trumpet vine (*Campsis radicans*) sprouting from runners in the grass, the mile-a-minute vine (*Persicaria perfoliata*) smothering my beloved blackberries on the sunny edge between woodland and meadow.

This summer, I declared war, donning indestructible Agway farmer gloves for my evening walks and ripping these spiny vines—known as tearthumb for good reason—from my favorite stands of berries.

Our sliver of woods, once so full of dogwood, mountain laurel, and sycamore, is choking on invasives: barberry, Russian olive, honeysuckle, multiflora rose, stilt grass—to name a few of the ornamentals that have escaped American gardens.

So now, when I see a sassafras seedling sprouting its mitten leaves in that unmown front yard, or a white oak nestled against the unshorn boxwood, I welcome them into my wild garden. I pull up the honeysuckle that inevitably appears, programmed to strangle the young trunks, and the mullein that could so easily steal moisture from baby roots. And a year or so later, on some cool, overcast day, I dig them up, very carefully, praying I won't snap the roots, and plant them around the farm.

Oaks, I learned from ecologist Doug Tallamy, support more than five hundred species of butterflies. Which is why I let the grass grow, and watch what seeds itself in. And what eats its leaves. And what eats it.

As long as they don't eat all my Brandywines, I'm happy.

ANNE RAVER is a garden commentator for WYPR Public Radio and for eleven years was a reporter and gardening columnist for the *New York Times*. She has covered topics as diverse as microbes in the soil; farmers struggling to preserve their land; growers devastated by hurricanes; and the medicinal uses of plants in the Amazon. She lives in central Maryland.

Saving Graces
Margaret Roach

It is no wonder so much of gardening is done on one's knees: the practice of horticulture is a wildly humbling way to pass the days on Earth. Even the root of the word "humility" comes from the Latin *humus* (for "earth" or "ground"), and a good soil is rich in the partially decayed plant and animal material we call that very thing. Humbled or no, "gardener" was the label imprinted on me when souls were handed out, and so be it. The challenge? To make that term cohabit inside me with "corporate publishing executive," the persona I'd taken on from my newspaper-executive father but not been born with.

The depth of my connection to gardening, my elemental urge to meld with other living things that do not yell or put forth unrealistic expectations, probably plotted my course to the rural New York State property where I now live, made it my magnetic north.

I survived the intensity of my corporate years by gardening on weekends with a vengeance (motivational Al Green CDs on the boombox beside me), buying any plants I craved. The garden quickly exceeded the capability of even me, one exceptionally hyperactive weekender with a highly effective long-handled round-point shovel I'd bought at a yard sale and no shortage of Monday-to-Friday issues to exorcise.

This gardening-frenzy-as-outlet didn't work in winter, however, as the average low temperature here in USDA Zone 5B is −15 (and −20 is not unfamiliar). For four or five months a year, there simply is no gardening allowed. The precious soil eludes me beneath a crusted moonscape fashioned by freeze-thaw weather and persistent winds—a surface I can often walk on, if I dare, without falling through, an icy deck erected over the garden, a giant baked Alaska. It was—and sometimes is—like being cut off from my most elemental self.

Gardening had been my refuge for many years by the time I moved to my present land, a hobby cultivated when my widowed mother, just forty-nine, became confused, and my only sister needed me to help sort things out. Investigation revealed the Alzheimer's and landed me back in my childhood home, cutting down the overgrown privet hedges and yews—a self-imposed occupational therapy by day, before evenings spent editing copy at the *New York Times*. Even then, when I had no botanical Latin or any confidence in what I was doing, gardening was my first moving meditation, my yoga. When I was raking, I raked—in the moment of raking awareness, neither thinking in shoulda-coulda-woulda monkey mind, nor wandering into daydreams, past or future. Being truly at attention and one with the task: that sense of perfect union was what I had not found anywhere else, and certainly not at work.

Later, when my mother could stay home no longer, and the house was gone, replaced by the weekend place, the first garden of my own, the same feeling overtook me: when I was weeding, I was really weeding. In those early years, I was in it as if it were the motions of a vinyasa—deepening my connection to the place, to this impossible piece of lopsided land.

To be a gardener is to come face to face with powerlessness (not something written anywhere in the corporate mission statements of any of my employers), and to cultivate patience as actively as you do plants. In spite of following all the directions gleaned from Grandma and from garden books, despite considerable years of hands-on experience and experiments and access to some of the most knowledgeable masters of the art, I know only one thing for certain about gardening now, thirty years in: things will die.

Oh, and usually they will do so just when they're really starting to look good, after heroic measures of love and many dollars spent, after you have grown very attached. Minimizing your losses isn't part of the picture.

The heavens will fail to provide manna in the form of rain and send violent, leaf-shredding hail instead. The neighbor's dog will piss on the treasure you grew from a cutting, and it will perish. *Where's my vining aconitum?* you wonder out loud, feeling vaguely ill; the mow-and-blow guys (if you can find anyone who will mow a tricky place like this—I cannot) will say they *thought it was a weed, lady,* and therefore whacked it (and very thoroughly at that: well done . . .).

The garden is where there's no pretending that living things don't die.

Whatever you don't kill makes you stronger, though, and hungrier for more plants and then some more, and so this bond deepens. Curiosity becomes interest, interest becomes hobby, hobby becomes passion, passion becomes life's work, and even spiritual pursuit—the stuff of the heart.

The Zen master speaks of chopping wood, carrying water. The gardener will know what it is to really be in the moment when she does her most rote, insistent chores. I know I do, and so I garden with a blend of horticultural how-to and woo-woo, and the views (both outward and inward) are better for it. I practiced horticultural excess, yes, before I quit my job and moved here full-time, but I also practiced communion and some moments of peace. In short: my garden saved me.

"Your garden is beautiful," people say when they come touring on garden open days. "How did it get this way?"

"This is what happens when you stay in one place for twenty years," I tell them, "and just keep digging more holes."

No, you don't end up in China, as my mom teased all those years ago. You end up right here, right now, speaking passable botanical Latin punctuated with some key Buddhist phrases for good measure—a bit of Hindi and a lot of *Hello, Baby, Mommy loves you* fusing into a delightful gibberish. Or at least it delights me. And the creatures (the frogs and birds and snakes and plants and cat) do not in any obvious manner appear to object.

MARGARET ROACH has been writing about gardening for more than twenty years. Previously she was garden editor at *Newsday* and then for Martha Stewart, where she was the first garden editor and later editorial director of *Martha Stewart Living*. She writes her blog, *A Way to Garden*, from her garden in upstate New York.

Right This Way
Marty Ross

If ever there was a gentler time, it was just the other day, when I was out in the garden doing as little as possible, tossing weeds from the flower beds onto the lawn, deadheading the daylilies, watering the tomatoes, and furtively rooting around the margins of the compost pile, hoping to see a box turtle. You never actually find them by looking for them, but I keep an eye out.

In the workaday world, distractions are a nuisance—focus is paramount—but in the garden, every distraction is a delight. On the way to check the asparagus (which is in trouble), I wander over to tap gently on a bluebird house to see if anyone is at home and then inspect the hollies for tiny green new berries and worry about their lone, hard-working pollinator, which really needs to be weeded around as soon as the opportunity presents itself—and suddenly it does. There are no bee-lines in my garden.

What a luxury it is to fill the bird feeders and pat the lily pads in the sun, give the beans an encouraging hand up their poles, and pinch a stem or two of parsley for the kitchen counter. Pushing a wheelbarrow full of compost across the lawn seems to lighten my load. Like every garden, mine is full of plans and things to do, but I do not much aspire to finish anything. I mean, I'm just getting started.

I am not a mother. "Aunt Marty" is close enough for me. But I have been nurturing plants since I first sowed radishes and zinnias in a flowerbed with my father at the age of four. I remain especially susceptible to small plants, to acorns, to boxwood cuttings, and to coming home from plant sales with grand magnolias in four-inch pots.

I do not name my plants, or think of them as "she" or "he," but I talk to them nevertheless, if wordlessly, while I work around them. One gets lost in these quiet conversations, but can never go astray, since there are really no wrong turns, just diversions. Gardening is a journey to nowhere in particular, and I'm on my way, trowel in hand.

I have my ideas and opinions about gardening, of course. There are certain things I am trying to achieve, and I sometimes manage to pull them off. I want my plants to thrive and my flower combinations to ring out lustily, but gardening is sometimes hard.

The franklinia is suddenly stone dead, for example. A friend in a high horticultural place warned me that this would happen. "They are extinct for a reason," he told me. *Franklinia alatamaha* is native to the banks of the Altamaha River in Georgia, but no wild specimens are known to exist. All franklinias in gardens today are said to be directly descended from trees grown by the eighteenth-century botanists John and William Bartram in their garden in Philadelphia. Mine came from the capable gardeners at Colonial Williamsburg, and it lived for about five years, during which time it grew taller than I am (this is not saying much, but it started off in a one-gallon pot), bloomed beautifully, and put on a magnificent show of fall color every year. It never even leafed out this spring. I planted a twelve-inch physocarpus in its place.

The losses are lamentable, but experimentation is my specialty. Even though I have two gardens twelve hundred miles and several hardiness zones apart, I am always running out of room, and the holes where experiments went awry never remain empty for long. I collect boxwoods, witch hazels, peonies, daffodils, deciduous hollies, and magnolias. It has pleased my husband to impose a strict limit on the collection of hostas, which he regards as frumpy, and officially, we are at ten. The unofficial count is around twenty-five cultivars.

I am also hungrily ambitious for my vegetable garden, but, in truth, it frequently has to fend for itself because I am often not around to pamper the lettuces or even pick the peppers. We reliably harvest a dozen or more butternut squash from vines that sprout in the compost heap every summer. We suspected a mysterious crop failure last fall, or perhaps a raccoon, but it turned out our neighbor had picked the squash for safekeeping while we were away: she delivered them in a big red Macy's shopping bag during the holidays—very festive indeed.

Fresh tomatoes are, of course, a fundamental part of the pleasure of backyard gardening, and I am a tomato gardener of the most dedicated sort, planting both early and late varieties. More or less as I write, I am grafting delicious heirloom 'Cherokee Purple' black tomatoes onto sturdy hybrid 'Celebrity' rootstock. This experiment, involving a razor blade, aquarium tubing, and some dexterity, took place at the pine table on the back porch, an indispensable garden annex. I dutifully studied a tomato-grafting video on YouTube and proceeded more or less according to the instructions, improvising where necessary (my father long ago taught me to cheat at such games). Two out of five grafts appear to have taken. This may change my life, at least until something new comes along.

I am not a competitive gardener. I stage my most impressive flower shows on the kitchen windowsill, twirling each stem between my fingers to find its best face and choosing just the right container from the array on either side of the faucet. The current inventory of vases includes a slim caper bottle, a couple of old-time spice bottles with skinny necks, an inkwell, and the 1916 Katz Trophy, a modest silver loving cup from Hot Springs Country Club. This second- or third-hand trophy was in fact awarded to my father, by me, in the 1980s, after he coached me through a difficult time at work. I didn't get the new assignment I sought, but I made my point, and recently my father awarded it back to me: I treasure this little early inheritance.

My garden is my escape, not so much from anything in particular as to everything else. I do an awful lot of gardening right here at my desk, and I flee from the keyboard and the screen to the sound of the wind in the trees, the song of the mockingbird and the cardinal, and the fragrance of mint, which is trying to take over a shady flowerbed by the porch; to rose hips and bird's nests, to the heft and slosh of watering cans, and, above all, to the unexpected. Yesterday, on my way back from checking on some hellebore seedlings and getting a few quick basil plants in the ground, I stood, nibbling on a pinch of tarragon, and followed a little hummingbird in her flight from the feeder, hoping to discover her nest. I lost her in the sparkle among the leaves. I looked down again, blinking, and there at my feet was a turtle. I don't pick them up, or put a mark on them so I'll know them the next time, although I occasionally take their pictures before they amble off into the shrubbery.

The race never goes to the swift in my garden: that sort of pace is frowned on here, but I am always making progress, and I expect I'll be encountering that same turtle among the ferns and the hollyhocks for a long, long time.

MARTY ROSS writes about gardens, people, and the history and culture of horticulture. Her monthly gardening column is syndicated by Universal UClick, and she writes regularly for the *Kansas City Star*. She is regional editor for *Better Homes and Gardens* and *Country Gardens*. She divides her time between gardens in Kansas City, Missouri, and Tidewater Virginia.

Sightings
Claire Sawyers

I garden for the serendipitous moments. Like the other day, sitting on my front porch and seeing a ruby-throated hummingbird zip up the front walk to visit the bee balm and check out a few franklinia blossoms before resting on a branch for a moment and then spinning up and over the house, top-like, out of sight. I also garden because I don't watch TV—at all. Instead, I have windows without curtains, and each season brings a new lineup. The bedroom drama stars black bamboo (not recommended for G audiences); in the spring, the shoots grow so fast they could be considered an action show.

Another reason I garden is that I want flowers or foliage brought inside, so there is something that speaks of the season. A vase in my small bathroom stays full (as in two to three feet full) most of the year (read *In Praise of Shadows* to understand this Japanese aesthetic). The blooms of *Rosa* 'Knock Out' seem to vibrate against its red walls, and I even sacrifice my lilies for the bathroom since I don't stake (although that has led to pollen-stained towels). A few quilted *Hosta* 'Sum and Substance' leaves do well there for a week or two; stems of variegated miscanthus, falling into the street after a heavy rain, come inside where they make an exuberant fountain, "spilling" into the shower for stretches of the autumn. A fine way for me to start a summer weekend is with a Friday evening circle around the garden, picking something for the bathroom—a simple ritual to detach from the workweek, a simple practice to become aware of botanical details that emerged during the week. Later, while I'm doing something as mundane as brushing my teeth, I notice, for example, the venation pattern of hydrangea leaves.

I garden because I love the empty, exhausted, but satisfied feeling that comes from using a shovel or rake all day or from moving wheelbarrow after wheelbarrow full of compost, although I don't enjoy the blisters. There is a tangible result from the effort exerted. Gardening produces something I can reflect on, sometimes with satisfaction, sometimes with frustration, but always there is something by which to measure progress. I garden for the physical joy of it, for the pleasure of the rhythms of the process. I dance for the same reason.

Both gardening and dancing are physical reactions and interpretations. In dancing I make music personal; in gardening I make my surroundings personal. I may not be great at either; but through the process I experience myself, I have a sense of self and creative expression. But dance, perhaps fortunately in my case, is a fleeting manifestation, while gardening leaves an observable trail to revisit.

I garden because I think it will get others to garden, too. As director of a public garden, I spend more time behind a computer now than I do behind a trowel, but indirectly I'm promoting gardening because I believe everyone would have a richer, more fulfilled life if they gardened. My home garden is on a corner lot and a block from a train station, so I hope to influence commuters on their way to the train and other passersby. Invariably when I'm in the garden, someone will roll down their car window to praise ("I love your garden") or question ("What is that vine on the street sign?"—at least I heard that during the years I grew *Dolichos lablab*, but that was before the township made me remove the wire support around the post). I answer, never revealing I'm a professional horticulturist; I want them to think, *If she can do this, so can I.*

My present lot is too shady for vegetables, but in the past I have picked places to live in order to grow vegetables. There is not much I can think of that provides more simple pleasure than growing my own food: picking my own raspberries, slurping up the juice from a plate of homegrown sliced tomatoes, chopping up a bundle of basil for pesto. My earliest gardening memories are of the large vegetable garden on my grandparents' Missouri farm. They entrusted me to plant beans and peas in rows with the guide of hay baler twine—important responsibility for a four-year-old. A photo from my teens shows me beaming, proudly holding a pair of Japanese cucumbers from my self-started vegetable garden; the decorated cake in the photo with me proclaims "1st cucumber day" with a couple of cucumber slices instead of icing-made roses.

While writing this essay I happened to read about Barton Seaver ("A Fisher of Men," *National Geographic Traveler*, October 2011). Once a chef, he now devotes his time to saving the fish of the oceans. Overfishing, as he sees it, stems from the fact that most of us no longer relate to oceans; where we used to have to cross them in ships, "now we board a plane, go to sleep and wake up on the other side. We've lost our connection." I garden to maintain that same sort of connection. No falling asleep while flying on this earth for me, please. Plants form the basis of all life I am a part of and dependent upon to survive; how can we not relate to plants?

Aren't we genetically predisposed to garden? Hasn't natural selection favored those who mastered gardening? They produced enough food to live. Isn't asking why I garden akin to asking why I have an opposable thumb or walk upright? Doesn't the ability to garden, to cultivate my own food, in part, define me as a species? I imagine many of us have a kind of residual propensity to garden. I imagine I garden because it is deeply embedded in my genetic code. With children increasingly averse simply to being outside, I wonder where that gene is going. The really interesting question is not "Why do I garden?" but rather "Why doesn't everyone garden?"

Since 1990, CLAIRE SAWYERS has been the director of the Scott Arboretum at Swarthmore College, Swarthmore, Pennsylvania. Prior to that she worked at Mt. Cuba Center for the Study of Piedmont Flora in Hockessin, Delaware. She has gardened in Japan, France, and Belgium in addition to the United States, and is the author of *The Authentic Garden*.

The Universal Itch
Amy Stewart

Let's sort out the grammar first. "Garden" is a verb, not a noun. A garden is not a thing you can buy or own or ever possibly finish. No, "garden" is something you do. It's an active, fidgety sort of pastime, another way of jingling the loose change in your pocket, except that the pocket happens to be your backyard, and the change is a hellebore, or a cherry tree.

So why do it? Apart from fire-building or stone-cutting, gardening may well be our oldest human enterprise. Picture a woman walking through a field of tall grass gone to seed. Most of the seed dropped to the ground when the stiff spikelets shattered. But a few grains still cling to the stalk. She thinks, "Hmmm. Could be good. Wonder if my kids will eat it." She pockets a few—well, maybe she doesn't have a pocket, maybe she has not yet invented the pocket, but she palms a few—and at that moment, barley enters domestication. Beer and bread cannot be far behind. From there comes music, cooking, and literature—and civilization is born.

Which is not to say that I am paying deliberate homage to some ancient Gaia figure every time I bring a pony pack of petunias home from the nursery. But I do believe that tinkering with the plant world is so primitive, so much a part of what makes us human, that it qualifies as more than a pastime. It is not golf or tennis. It is not knitting. It is not, in spite of what backyard makeover television shows would have us believe, a type of home décor. No, gardening is how we interact with the plant kingdom. The one that makes the air we breathe and the food we eat and the medicine we take when we're sick and miserable.

And we're all gardeners once in a while, aren't we? Now and then? Given the opportunity? I have yet to meet anyone who hasn't once poured water on a plant to make it grow or yanked a weed out of the ground to make room for something better. Any urbanite, any sophisticate, any hedge fund manager, can remember a day, back in his indiscriminate youth, when he might have once dug a hole in the ground and set something alive in there. The question of why I garden becomes rather insignificant when we acknowledge that we all garden, a little bit.

As fidgeting goes, gardening is particularly remunerative. Take weeding. A single pass through the garden can be made in the morning with one hand holding a cup of coffee (or a gin and tonic, if it's the afternoon) while the other hand dislodges a few weeds. There's something about this fussy behavior that I find more calming than yoga. Just a few minutes out there are enough to clear the head, not to mention the rhubarb patch.

Digging in the dirt is even more rewarding, this being an opportunity to come into direct contact with the planet and its many mysteries. There are worms down there, and voles, and mites and springtails and a billion other creatures we can't fathom. I wonder why anyone pays good money to go whale watching when there are nightcrawlers to be uncovered in the rose bed. Even turning over a rock is bound to inspire an idea about something: warfare, motherhood, sowbugs. The plots of novels have been conceived while turning the compost pile—I'm sure of it.

Pruning and deadheading are equally satisfying. Grooming is an even earlier human enterprise than gardening. I like to pick the lint off sweaters, and I have always hoped that some child of a friend would turn up with lice so I could volunteer to pour oil over her head and comb out the nits. I like to extract the poppy seeds from muffin tins, and I enjoy popping the seedheads off perennials. Few activities are more thrilling and addictive than taking a large rake and combing the dead strands out of bone-dry blue fescue. I have worn a clump of grass nearly to death with this treatment.

So there it is: gardening gives us something to pick at, and for the most part, a garden likes to be picked at and does even better afterward. But is that all?

No. There's another important reason to garden. I garden to find a place to put the plants I've bought. Gardening is the obligatory second phase to shopping. This may sound obvious: what else would you do with a plant after you've bought it, besides put it in the ground? But I know people who have neither the time nor the room to plant everything they buy. Their driveways become so cluttered with black plastic pots that the neighbors mistake them for a nursery and show up on Saturday afternoons with a wagon and a roll of small bills.

At the garden center, every plant represents possibility. A tomato with fruit that tastes of tangerines? A purple coleus with chartreuse fringe? I'll take three. I buy these plants having no idea where they might go, whether they will thrive in my chilly maritime climate, or if they will survive my misguided and careless ministrations. I just buy them. I'm not into shoes or lipstick or fast cars. I'm into palm leaf begonias, because they are madcap Victorian creations that bring to mind dirigibles, Paris green wallpaper, and opium dens. I garden because I can't help myself.

AMY STEWART is the author of five books on the perils and pleasures of the natural world. She has appeared on hundreds of national and regional radio and television programs, and has written for the *New York Times*, the *San Francisco Chronicle*, and many national garden magazines. Her most recent book is *Wicked Bugs*. She lives in Eureka, California.

Fruit Loops
Roger B. Swain

"I would have bet a considerable amount of money," said the editor from the *New York Times*, "that the word 'frugivorousness' was not a word. I would have been wrong." His concession (one that I, a former editor, still treasure) concerned a brief essay that I'd written about my childhood construction of a fruit-filled cornucopia to accompany my family's Thanksgiving meal. This display stretched the length of the table and encompassed a botanical range matched only by the diversity of guests that could be gathered in a university town. My centerpiece was not meant to be decorative; I meant it to be eaten as soon the noonday meal had settled. Indeed, I intended to be first in line.

We call meat-eaters carnivores. If it's seeds you prefer, you are a granivore. A diet of bugs makes you an insectivore. Anyone who has eaten his or her way through an

entire Thanksgiving dinner should be labeled an omni-
vore. But fruit is what I like to eat, first and foremost.
Put me down, then, as frugivorous.

Currant and raspberry jelly fueled my New England
childhood. My mother liked to process the fruits that
she picked, so our fruit-room shelves were filled with
marmalades, chutneys, sauces and other preserves. My
father, on the other hand, preferred to put any fruit that
he encountered directly into his mouth. As for me, no
wild grapes were too high, no blackberries too thorny,
no little green apples too tart. Even the wild strawberries were fair game, the ones so small that you had to
pick eighteen to make a dozen. What couldn't be found
afield came from the grocery store. There what beck-
oned was the exotic—the red bananas, mangos, kum-
quats, and pomegranates—a most intemperate harvest.

Growing up on mixed fruit, however, is not the
same as setting out to raise one's own. In this regard
I bloomed late. I didn't start gardening intently until
my sixteenth birthday. In the mid-1960s, marijuana
patches were where many got their horticultural start.
I veered off and pursued competitive vegetable growing instead. I was encouraged in this by Fletcher Wason,
a man some fifty years my senior, who collected and
exhibited heirloom potatoes, and who timed his plantings not according to the first and last frosts, but by the
dates of the Hillsborough County Fair. Fletcher lived

a couple of towns away from me here in southern New Hampshire, and we met once a year to compete, our exhibits laid out on tables inside a grass-carpeted tent.

On one of those bright September days, flanked by long rows of picture-perfect vegetables, Fletcher, white-haired and quite deaf, roared at me, "Have you got your fruit in yet?" I had to admit that I hadn't, and I could see he had a point. Radishes may be ready twenty-eight days from sowing. Not fruit. So I went home, dug up still more ground and ordered a bed of strawberries. Next came raspberries, blueberries, and the first grape-vines. Soon, my father and I fenced an acre of pasture and set out an assortment of apples, pears, and stone fruits (those with a pit, like cherries).

Tree fruits, other than peaches, take years to mature, and by the mid '70s this orchard was still in its infancy. I was commuting between garden and graduate school when I met Elisabeth Ward. She was an Italian Renaissance historian at Harvard, but her first valentine to me contained Andrew Marvell's line "my vegetable love should grow." And it did, but left alone in her Cambridge apartment one afternoon, I absentmindedly ate everything out of her fruit bowl only to discover upon her return that we differed about the proper rate of consumption for a centerpiece. It was our first argument. What settled it, and assured our amicable future, was not my offer to refill the bowl but the discovery that as a teenager in Pittsburgh she had won a week of vocational testing, which revealed, the examiners said, a "surprising interest in pomology." Fruit growing was to be us.

Shortly thereafter there were also paintings on the wall—the portraits of the founders of the Massachusetts Horticultural Society. These were a few steps from my desk at *Horticulture* magazine, where I'd landed a job as science editor in the society's three-story brick building across the street from Boston's Symphony Hall. The outside was decorated with garlands of carved stone fruit, the inside with oil paintings of stern nineteenth-century gentlemen who had owned great estates around Boston, men with gardens outdoors and under glass, men who grew fruit.

The history of American horticulture begins with fruit, and if you page through a bound issue of the society's *Transactions*, you can't miss it. Here are the reports of annual festivals dating back to 1829. You can see who brought the "orange trees in fruit and flower," "the trellis of grapes raised in the open air," "pears—34 kinds, many of them new," "a muskmelon weighing 19½ pounds." All these, the recording secretary reassures us, were arranged "in a very chaste and appropriate manner."

These displays were accompanied by dinners. While the various toasts that were presented at each of these are duly chronicled, there is no record of the menus. I think we can safely say that some of what they ate was the fruit on display. Not all of it, perhaps. The home-grown pineapples, the fruit that was becoming synonymous with New England hospitality, may have been spared, but the rest got eaten, or got carried home to be eaten shortly thereafter. It had to be.

The fact is that you can be frugivorous without raising fruit, but not the other way around. Now that I am the age of those who once stared down upon me from the walls of the president's gallery, now that my hair and beard are turning white, I understand fruit better than ever.

For instance, unless you raise your own fruit, you don't have the real thing. Those fruits we bring home from the store are unripe. They have to be. Ripeness and decay are so closely linked that ripe fruit can't be shipped. Some of the immature fruit we buy—the pears, for example—may get tastier in due course, but most fruit never will or never can. If it's eye appeal you are looking for, then you might as well fill your fruit bowl with artificial fruit. At least that way your mouth won't be disappointed.

The only way to discover what fruit should actually taste like is to raise it yourself, waiting to pick a peach until your fingers leave a mark as you pull it from the branch, or until the wasps are competing with you for the grapes. This is the point at which the fruit is truly ready. But this moment comes with a built-in deadline. It needs to be eaten now.

Fletcher was right to tell me to get my fruit in. Perhaps he sensed my frugivorousness. Perhaps he knew it would give me the patience to wait for the individual plants to mature and actually start bearing. Perhaps he knew the role that fruit had played in the lives of those early horticulturists. I know what it has meant in mine. All gardening is productive. If you don't have a surplus at the end of a season, you have done something terribly wrong. But fruit growing is the most productive of all. Nothing is surer to inspire generosity. You may start out to raise fruit just for yourself, but you can't escape the philanthropy that ensues. Some of the fruit will invariably need to be given away. Don't think surplus zucchini. This is way better than that. No one ever turns down a basket of cherries, a bag of plums. Fruit is guaranteed to make you friends. This is my orchard, my vineyard, my berry patch—my social network.

The author of five books, ROGER B. SWAIN is known as "the man with the red suspenders." From the mid-1980s until 2001 he hosted the television show *The Victory Garden* on PBS, and from 1978 until 2008 he was a writer and science editor at *Horticulture* magazine. He lectures on a wide variety of garden-related topics. He lives in Massachusetts and New Hampshire.

The Web
Douglas W. Tallamy

Most people garden because they love plants, but I garden because I love animals—all kinds of animals. Animals with two legs (birds), four legs (box turtles, salamanders, and foxes), six legs (butterflies and beetles), eight legs (spiders), dozens of legs (centipedes), hundreds of legs (millipedes), and even animals with no legs (snakes and pollywogs). I admit that I am not evenhanded or commonplace in my love of animals: birds get the nod over rabbits, groundhogs, and deer; and I appreciate the extraordinary diversity and importance of insects more than most gardeners do. It's not that I don't appreciate the beauty of plants; I certainly do. And I am grateful for their ability to sequester carbon, filter and store water, clean and cool air, build and hold soil, and make the oxygen that I breathe every minute of every day.

But I like plants mostly for what they do for my precious animals. The plants in my garden make the food that enables all the animals in our yard to exist. Those plants make the leaves that feed hundreds of species of caterpillars. They produce the pollen that enables dozens of species of bees to reproduce in our yard and the nectar that fuels the flight of at least thirty species of butterflies and skippers. Our garden plants provide the seeds that supply the needs of large and small beetle species and the leaf litter that enriches and protects the diverse communities of life within our soil. And the plants that my wife and I have added to our property have, in a few short years, increased the number of breeding bird species from eleven to well over fifty. At least fifteen additional avian species can now use our garden as a place to rest and refuel during their spring and fall migrations.

I garden the way I garden—with a heavy bias toward plants that have been part of local food webs for millennia—because that is the only way the natural world I love is able to thrive in our yard. When we moved to our property—part of an abandoned hay field—it was overrun with invasive Asian plants. I knew that in order to see local animals, we would have to restore their habitat and the food webs that sustain them. Hence, our use of plants that share the sun's energy with other creatures.

Encouraging animals that feed on our plants does not

endanger the garden. Native insects attracted to the garden provide the food for many animals that eat insects—the minute parasitic wasps that reproduce within the eggs of stink bugs and caterpillars, the larger wasps that develop within the bodies of caterpillars and beetles, the assassin bugs and ambush bugs that help control fall webworms and treehoppers, the damsel bugs that eat plant bug eggs, the jumping spiders that pounce on unsuspecting leafhoppers, the viruses that turn caterpillars into mush, the big-headed flies that make sure we don't have too many planthoppers, the small-headed flies that make sure we don't have too many spiders, the thick-headed flies that make sure we don't have too many paper wasps, and above all, the birds, which eat insects from dawn to dusk.

Gardening with native plants has been criticized as little more than an emotional longing for a romanticized past. Although I have defended my preference for native plants many times, with both science and what seems to me like common sense (animals need to eat), there is no denying that I am motivated by emotion. To watch the daily lives of other species, and to know that these creatures survive because of my gardening choices, brings me feelings of accomplishment, satisfaction, joy, and wonder, and even an occasional paternal glow.

A blooming crape myrtle seen against a blue sky is undeniably beautiful; a weeping blue atlas cedar, its branches sweeping the ground, is striking; and forsythia is a remarkably reliable herald of spring. Yet these plants do not support the food webs of North America, and when there is no food, animals must go elsewhere to live. I take satisfaction in knowing that, with so few "elsewheres" left, animals can find food and shelter in our yard. Besides, in my mind, crape myrtles are not as beautiful as the cecropia moth that develops on my native cherry trees; a blue atlas cedar can't match the magic of the bolas spider, which mimics the sex pheromone of its moth prey in order to attract them to its sticky bolas. And nothing is as dependable as the blue grosbeak male that sings at the top of my white pine at 7 a.m. every day from June through August because he has enough food to support a mate and raise his family.

I garden the way I garden because I would not be whole without these creatures in my life.

DOUGLAS W. TALLAMY teaches at the University of Delaware, in Newark. He is a professor and the chair of the entomology and wildlife ecology department there, where he has been studying insects and their role in the environment for more than twenty years. He is the author of *Bringing Nature Home*.

Urban Gardener
Richard G. Turner, Jr.

Even as a young child, I was drawn to two extremes: the excitement of the big city and the wonder of nature. Back in the early 1950s, Detroit *was* a big city, and I thrilled to the crowds of people, the cacophony of automobiles and streetcars, grand movie palaces, J. L. Hudson's giant department store, Sanders chocolate shops, and those wonderfully tall buildings spearing the sky.

Yet I was equally fascinated by the trees, flowers, birds, and bugs that could be found throughout the residential neighborhoods. My parents maintained a small vegetable garden and charged me (at age five) with monitoring the climbing beans. I watched them every day, making sure that their rapidly elongating shoots always found a string to grab, and was thrilled to harvest edible beans as the season progressed. The two nurses who lived next door introduced me to their much more elaborate garden. Maxine, in particular, spent hours with me after school and on weekends, teaching me about plants and gardens.

On my eighth birthday, we moved to the far eastside suburbs, to a tract home with a larger yard than we had had in the city. By the age of nine, I was given charge of the entire garden—but with the most minimal of budgets. I solicited divisions of plants from the few neighbors who gardened and spent my meager allowance on a pot of primroses that I immediately divided. Spring bulbs held a particular appeal. I loved planting them as the leaves were dropping in autumn, knowing that in spring the garden would be full of flowers as soon as the snow melted. At least that was my vision. In fact, since I bought only a few bulbs at a time, the effect was more in my mind than in reality. I've always wondered if the folks at Mitsch Novelty Daffodils in Oregon knew that a preteen was ordering those three bulbs each fall.

I spent most of my time outdoors, both in the garden and in the remnant woods, swamps, and creeks of our rapidly expanding community—capturing as many small life forms as possible to study at close range; keeping track of the birds that passed through the garden during the fall and spring migrations; and recording the first sprout or blossom of spring and the last leaf-drop of fall. I tried to recreate a wild landscape in a corner of the yard, by "rescuing" wildflowers and shrubs from the neighborhood woodlot (which soon fell to more housing). The birds were especially drawn to that section of the garden.

When it came time to go to college, however, I chose to study architecture, so I could learn more about those big buildings downtown. At school in Ann Arbor, I discovered landscape design and urban planning, fields where trees and other living things were as important as the people-centric elements. After a couple years working for architects, I returned for a masters in landscape architecture and was fortunate to secure a job in the campus landscape architect's office while in school and for several years after. I loved creating landscapes on the campus and encouraging the natural vegetation to reestablish on the university's north campus. But I did not have a garden of my own, and craved an opportunity to garden year-round.

I escaped Michigan and moved to San Francisco, drawn by its big-city architecture, its proximity to the country, and its year-round gardening climate. Lacking a real garden at first, I volunteered in the nursery at Strybing Arboretum, where I met gardeners with a wealth of knowledge about plants and gardens of the Bay Area. The arboretum was also a setting for bird and animal life of all types, proving that wildlife can exist in the city.

I dreamed of a place where I could have both a view of the city skyline and a private garden. I began doodling an apartment on the top floor of a building of three or four stories, built into a hill so that there would be a city view on one side and a garden on the opposite side, stretching even further up the hill. On a brilliantly sunny October morning in 1981, I found it, and I have been there ever since.

From the living room, the view includes the bay and two bridges, the distant East Bay Hills and Mount Diablo (thirty miles east), and the full expanse of the city skyline. To the rear, a private garden begins at the flat's fourth-floor level and rises another two stories; from the top of the garden the view opens to the city skyline again. The garden is modest. A steep pitch limits access to a few goat trails, but the soils are well drained and moderately rich. I've filled it with plants that will attract wildlife, especially hummingbirds, and I've tested the limits of gardening without water in the neighborhood's almost fog-free (and frost-free) climate. The garden has provided me with a classroom and a playground for experimenting with plants. It is full of wild critters, the vast majority of which benefit the plantings by keeping pests at bay. And it provides an antidote to the intensity of the big city, as well as an escape from the pressures of work.

I wouldn't want to live without the dynamic nature of

the big city, but I couldn't survive without the calming effect of nature in my own piece of paradise.

A garden designer, educator, writer, photographer, and tour leader, RICHARD G. TURNER, JR., studied architecture and landscape architecture at the University of Michigan before moving to California's Bay Area in order to garden year-round. From 1997 to 2012, Turner was editor of *Pacific Horticulture*, one of the top garden magazines in the United States.

Simple Pleasures
David Wheeler

To paraphrase Descartes: I garden, therefore I am. For more than six decades I've been fiddling around on the Earth's crust, and the pleasure of such activity has only increased in succeeding years. I now work an eight-acre piece of paradise with a partner who's equally committed. A blissful union, you might think, but gardeners can be just as independent and single-minded as painters, poets, or mountaineers. While we necessarily share certain chores and responsibilities (and, yes, occasionally, rely on outside help) we each have our own territory, parts of the garden we guard jealously and maintain to whatever standard we wish.

It's more difficult to say *why* I garden, than *how*. The whole horticultural world fascinates me, yet other interests must also be accommodated. Friendships need time, as does travel (not recommended for someone with living plants to nurture); gastronomy, cookery, and the pursuit of fine wine engage me; picture galleries beckon; and I'd struggle to keep my equilibrium without large daily doses of music—orchestral, chamber, opera, or simply the sound of a perfectly tuned piano.

As a young man, hard labour ruled my gardening life. I recall endless hours of digging and planting and falling into bed at sundown, exhausted by the glorious fatigue of extreme muscular exertion. I now find gardening's mental aspect equally stimulating (and often as demanding): new books and plantsmans' catalogues must be read, manuscripts need editing, while all the time an uncontrollable plant-collector's gene refuses to relax.

Simon and I garden in northwest Herefordshire, and the river on the southern edge of our five-acre arboretum marks the boundary between England and Wales. I started my tree collection on the first day of the new millennium by planting *Acer davidii* and a few snowdrops on the cold raked-over ashes of the previous night's bonfire. Since then I've added some four hundred trees and shrubs from around the temperate world, concentrating on autumn splendour. I've made small collections of prunus, liquidambar, sorbus, malus, and maple, and in recent years, as the trees have grown, I've underplanted them with hydrangea, aronia, viburnum, species roses, and a motley assortment of other smaller-growing shrubs. They in turn have wild flowers and bulbs beneath their skirts. The planting of all this was hugely satisfying, but the planning and plotting—nocturnal porings over encyclopedias in an armchair beside a blazing hearth or tucked under a mound of blankets as frost veined the bedroom windows—was equally rewarding. Is *that* why I garden?

On my first visit to North Hill in Vermont, some twenty years ago, I remember Wayne Winterrowd telling me how he and his partner Joe Eck would call plant names to each other at night, from one upstairs room to another. Simon and I can conversationally cruise for hours during meals or on long car journeys, pondering new plants, discussing changes to existing parts of the garden, contemplating entirely new schemes, reminiscing over past triumphs or disasters, inhabiting a private world to which no one else holds a key. The garden is under our fingernails, and the more we bury ourselves in its day-to-day practicalities, the more deeply we are embedded. I can't say I garden because of this unlikely camaraderie, but it is another part of the reason.

Much of gardening is sheer hard work, and to the uninitiated it might seem painfully monotonous or boring. Why would anyone in their right mind want to spend hours brushing snow off the branches of trees on freezing winter days, or stand for hours with a hosepipe in the afternoon heat of a summer drought? Why do we crawl about on stony ground pulling weeds or stand bent for hours, forking over the soil? Why do any of us trek hither and yon with barrowloads of muck to distribute among our treasured roses? Why all this pruning, watering, hoeing, raking, deadheading, sowing, reaping, mowing, staking, fertilizing . . . ?

Here's why: to watch a frail seedling become a tree where birds will one day perch and build their nests; to marvel at the gossamer emergence of a simple poppy; to sniff the riotous perfume of an exotic lily whose feral cousins lie in remote Himalayan valleys; to pick a basket of dewy fruit and vegetables bursting with the kind of flavours to which supermarkets can only aspire; to delve into the mysterious world of botany and science and speculate in some small way on creation and evolution; to bask in the sound of soil-refreshing rain on a hot summer's night or revel in the shade of a vine-clothed arbor at the end of a working day; to share with friends the beauty of Nature, however contrived; to smell and handle a fistful of brown dirt and understand whence we came and to what we will doubtless return.

In 1891, British gardener John Sedding wrote, "A well-kept garden makes credible to modern eyes the antique fable of an unspoiled world." He went on to trump himself by saying, "To own a bit of ground, to scratch it with a hoe, to plant seeds, and watch their renewal of life—this is the commonest delight of the race, the most satisfactory thing a man can do."

I agree, but it's more likely that I garden because I just don't know how to stop.

DAVID WHEELER is the editor of the British gardening quarterly *Hortus*, which he founded in 1987. He writes regularly for several British and international newspapers and magazines and tends an eight-acre garden and arboretum, Bryan's Ground, in Herefordshire.

The essay "Saving Graces" is adapted from *And I Shall Have Some Peace There* by Margaret Roach. Copyright 2011 by Margaret Roach. By permission of Grand Central Publishing.

Published in 2012 by Timber Press, Inc.

The Haseltine Building
133 S.W. Second Avenue, Suite 450
Portland, Oregon 97204-3527
timberpress.com

2 The Quadrant
135 Salusbury Road
London NW6 6RJ
timberpress.co.uk

Printed in the United States of America
Designed by Susan Applegate

Library of Congress Cataloging-in-Publication Data

The roots of my obsession: thirty great gardeners reveal why they garden/Thomas C. Cooper, editor.—1st ed.
   p. cm.
ISBN-13: 978-1-60469-271-6
1. Gardening—Anecdotes. I. Cooper, Thomas C.
SB455.W528 2012
635dc23   2011050643

A catalog record for this book is available from the British Library.